Super 7:

A Simple Bible Study with Teens or Youth as Leaders; For Families and/or Small Groups

by

Mary Ella Throener

DORRANCE
PUBLISHING CO
EST. 1920
PITTSBURGH, PENNSYLVANIA 15238

Dorrance Publishing Co
585 Alpha Drive
Pittsburgh, PA 15238
Visit our website at *www.dorrancebookstore.com*

ISBN: 978-1-6495-7079-6
eISBN: 978-1-6495-7019-2

INTRODUCTION

What is Super Seven?
It is a simple homemade Bible study for church groups,
the family and/or for independent study.

Why did I do this? Over the years in working with children and adults in Religious Education, I have seen a great need for all of us to have a deeper knowledge and connection with the Bible. What better education is there?

What are your favorite messages from the Bible? It was not all that many years ago that I would hesitate to answer that question.

In the Old Testament, my favorite Bible story is "Noah's Ark". The favorite verse from Psalm 23 is: "The Lord is my shepherd; there is nothing I shall want." I need reminders not to want food or money and thus be distracted from the real goal of: "treasures in heaven".

In the New Testament, my favorite Bible story is "Zacchaeus". My verse that speaks loud and clear and the one I need to pay attention to is: "Whoever has ears, ought to hear." Matthew 13:43

The Bible is the best book in the whole world. This simple Bible study is a tool to help the participants to be engaged in learning through questions and responses as well as homemade Bible games.

We begin our gatherings with spontaneous prayer, formal prayer and a song. Presently, the favorite song is "Me and God" by Josh Turner. Several other songs are also great to begin with to help us get a good focus on what we are about to encounter.

As we look at the Books with the Gospel questions, you will see that four or five questions are primarily about the content of that chapter. One question is usually a comparison between the Old Testament and the New Testament. Sometimes it is with two verses in different books of the New Testament. This is such an awesome awareness that I hadn't noticed for years!!! One or two questions are more personal because in reading God's Word, the Bible, we hope to develop a deeper relationship with God.

The homemade Bible games are to help us learn in a way that lifts our human hearts and inspires us to become better and strive for holiness!! In families, young children can become the leaders. They can read the questions, make the prizes, and lead the games. What an enjoyable activity to help unite the family and the church! Participants are expected to write their responses and reflections in their books. When we involve ourselves as human beings, especially our senses, we are gaining a deeper learning experience. The more we engage ourselves, the more we have the opportunity to integrate the good into our everyday lives. A guideline is for students in third grade or below to write the number of the verse down in their response and/or a word, fourth grade through sixth to write a few more words and all other participants to write sentences or as much as possible according to their abilities.

Selecting a certain time of the day or evening to do this as a family with a change of the designated leader will keep it interesting. Do you want this for your church group and/or family?

WHAT IF???

What if... all parishes of the diocese and country had the majority of their youth and parents reading and reflecting on the Word of God in the Bible?

What if...they greatly enjoyed it and wanted more?

Would this be a better place to live?

Would the daily news change for the better?

Would families be more united?

It is my hope and prayer.

Mary Ella Throener
methroener@hotmail.com
Resources used: "The New American Bible", Catholic World Press
                "The Catechism of the Catholic Church"

WHY?

Why do we read and study the Bible?

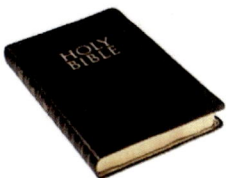

2 Timothy 3:16
We can know, love and serve God better, when we read His Book!

We begin this Bible Study with a focus statement. It is at the top of every page and we begin the questions and reflections after we have read a chapter in the Bible.

We read the selected Bible verse from the chapter together. It is suggested that we might choose to memorize this verse. Why do we memorize? We memorize important things in our life so that it becomes a part of who we are and what we believe.

We answer the questions that are primarily about the content of the chapter.

We answer the question of comparison. It is so fascinating that there are so many Old Testament Bible verses and New Testament verses that are alike or similar.

We answer some questions that ask for our personal thoughts and feelings in reflecting on the passage.

We personally write to God what we are thankful for at this moment and anything else we want to communicate with God. This is to foster our relationship with God! This is time to talk to our best friend ever!

SUPER SEVEN

The Holy Bible is:

The Word of God

Blueprint In-living Before Leaving Earth

Sacred Scripture

A Recipe on How to Live

A Divine Book

The Most Important Book in the World

The Good Book

• • •

The Old Testament and the New Testament

73 Books in the Catholic Bible

46 Books in the Old Testament

27 Books in the New Testament

THE BIBLE IS

THE WORD OF GOD

SUPER 7:
OPTIONAL GROUP SCHEDULE

3 or 4 hours each

Bible Verse Ball Game
Song
Bible: read, reflect and respond (2 chapters)
Can You Get 7?
7 Sacraments
Bible: read, reflect and respond (2 chapters)
Bible Verse Ladder Game
7 Capital Sins
Books of the Bible Relay Game

Bible Verse Ball Game
Song
Bible: read, reflect and respond (2 chapters)
7 Unities
Memory Card Game
Bible: read, reflect and respond (2 chapters)
7 Days of Creation
Bible Bingo
Books of the Bible Relay Game

SUPER 7:
OPTIONAL FAMILY SCHEDULE

(The Domestic Church)

Two games after reading two chapters would seem to work, but this could be a family choice to include one chapter and one game. Each family and each time slot would make a difference on what works best.

TABLE OF CONTENTS

FOCUS ON THE "WORD" WITH REFLECTIONS AND QUESTIONS

If the Word of God is in our mind, we hope the Word of God is in our heart.

Memory Verse: Please study and memorize.

Matthew: 1:1

"The book of the genealogy of Jesus Christ, the son of David, the son of Abraham."

QUESTIONS AND RESPONSES

1. How many generations are there from Abraham to the Messiah?

2. What does the word genealogy mean?

3. Who is the Messiah?

4. What does betrothed mean?

5. What dream is in the Old Testament: Genesis 37:5-11?

6. What was an important message in this chapter?

7. After reading and reflecting on this chapter, what do I want to thank God for?

If the Word of God is in our mind,
we hope the Word of God is in our heart.

Memory Verse: Please study and memorize.

Matthew: 2:23

"He went and dwelt in a town called Nazareth, so that what had been spoken through the prophets might be fulfilled, "He shall be called a Nazorean,"

QUESTIONS AND RESPONSES

1. Who are the Magi?

2. Where did Joseph and Mary go in order to be safe from King Herod?

3. What did King Herod do that was evil?

4. What is written in the Old Testament: Numbers 24:17 that is like Matthew 2:2 in the New Testament?

5. In the New Testament, Matthew 2:20 is parallel with the verse in the Old Testament, Exodus 4:19. What is this verse about?

6. What was an important message in this chapter?

7. After reading and reflecting on this chapter, what do I want to thank God for?

If the Word of God is in our mind,
we hope the Word of God is in our heart.

Memory Verse: Please study and memorize.

Matthew: 3:11

"I am baptizing you with water, for repentance, but the one who is coming after me is mightier than I."

QUESTIONS AND RESPONSES

1. What does it mean to repent?

2. What does it mean to produce good fruit?

3. In what river were a lot of people including Jesus baptized?

4. Who was John the Baptist?

5. What is written in the Old Testament, Psalm 2:7, that relates to this chapter?

6. What was an important message in this chapter?

7. After reading and reflecting on this chapter, what do I want to thank God for?

If the Word of God is in our mind, we hope the Word of God is in our heart

Memory Verse: Please study and memorize.

Matthew: 4:9

He said to them, "Come after me, and I will make you fishers of men."

QUESTIONS AND RESPONSES

1. How long did Jesus fast in the desert?

2. Who tested Jesus in the desert?

3. Who are the four apostles called in Matthew 4:18-22?

4. What did Jesus do in Galilee?

5. How is the verse from the Old Testament: Exodus 24:18 similar to Matthew 4:2?

6. What was an important message in this chapter?

7. After reading and reflecting on this chapter, wbat do I want to thank God for?

If the Word of God is in our mind,
we hope the Word of God is in our heart.

Memory Verse: Please study and memorize.
Matthew: 5:16
"Just so, your light must shine before others, that they may see your good deeds and glorify your heavenly Father."

QUESTIONS AND RESPONSES

1. The Sermon on the Mount is called what?

2. Whoever breaks one of the least of the commandments and teaches others to do so, is called what?

3. What advice have we been given about taking an oath?

4. What advice have we been given about loving our enemies?

5. How is Exodus 20:13 (Old Testament) like Matthew 5:21 (New Testament)?

6. What was an important message in this chapter?

7. After reading and reflecting on this chapter, what do I want to thank God for?

If the Word of God is in our mind, we hope the Word of God is in our heart

Memory Verse: Please study and memorize.

Matthew: 6:21

"For where your treasure is, there also your heart is."

QUESTIONS AND RESPONSES

1. What is almsgiving?

2. What prayer is in this chapter that we say at Mass?

3. What does it mean: "Where your treasure is, there also your heart is"?

4. What are we to seek first each and every day of our lives?

5. How is the verse in Matthew 6:16 in the New Testament like Leviticus 16:29 in the Old Testament?

6. What was an important message in this chapter?

7. After reading and reflecting on this chapter, what do I want to thank God for?

If the Word of God is in our mind,
we hope the Word of God is in our heart.

Memory Verse: Please study and memorize.

Matthew: 7:12

"Do to others whatever you would have them do to you. This is the law and the prophets."

QUESTIONS AND RESPONSES

1. Are we to ask God for things?

2. What is the Golden Rule?

3. What gate are we to choose the narrow or the wide? Why?

4. Who will be like a wise man who built his house on rock?

5. Why is the Psalm 6:9 in the Old Testament like Matthew 7:23 in the New Testament?

6. What was an important message in this chapter?

7. After reading and reflecting on this chapter, what do I want to thank God for?

If the Word of God is in our mind,
we hope the Word of God is in our heart.

Memory Verse: Please study and memorize.
Matthew: 8:19b
"Teacher, I will follow you wherever you go."

QUESTIONS and RESPONSES

1. Who had faith in this chapter of Matthew?

2. What does it mean when it says that Peter's mother-in-law was cured?

3. When were the apostles terrified? What did Jesus do?

4. Who preached and worked miracles in Galilee?

5. How are the verses in Matthew 8:1-4 in the New Testament like the verses in Leviticus 14:2-9 in the Old Testament?

6. What was an important message in this chapter?

7. After reading and reflecting on this chapter, what do I want to thank God for?

If the Word of God is in our mind,
we hope the Word of God is in our heart.

Memory Verse: Please study and memorize.
Matthew: 9:13
"Go and learn the meaning of the words, "I desire mercy, not sacrifice." I did not come to call the righteous but sinners."

QUESTIONS and RESPONSES

1. What disciple did Jesus tell: "Follow me"?

2. What kind of people did Jesus eat with?

3. Name two healings that Jesus performed?

4. What healing of Jesus, do you like the best?

5. Daniel 12:2 in the Old Testament is like Matthew 9:24 in the New Testament, in what way?

6. What was an important message in this chapter?

7. After reading and reflecting on this chapter, what do I want to thank God for?

If the Word of God is in our mind,
we hope the Word of God is in our heart.

Memory Verse: Please study and memorize.
Matthew: 10:16
"Behold I am sending you like sheep in the midst of wolves; so be shrewd as serpents and simple as doves."

QUESTIONS and RESPONSES

1. Name the twelve apostles.

2. What is the proclamation that Jesus asks the apostles to give?

3. What are we to have if someone insults us for believing in Jesus?

4. Who is being mentioned in Matthew 10:41?

5. Compare Exodus 4:12 in the Old Testament to Matthew 10:20 in the New Testament,

6. What was an important message in this chapter?

7. After reading and reflecting on this chapter, what do I want to thank God for?

If the Word of God is in our mind, we hope the Word of God is in our heart.

Memory Verse: Please study and memorize.

Matthew: 11:28

"Come to me, all you who labor and are burdened, and I will give you rest."

QUESTIONS and RESPONSES

1. Who is John the Baptist?

2. Who ate with tax collectors and sinners?

3. What did Jesus give to the Father?

4. What are we to take to Jesus in prayer?

5. What is being said in the Old Testament, Jeremiah 6:16?

6. What was an important message in this chapter?

7. After reading and reflecting on this chapter, what do I want to thank God for?

If the Word of God is in our mind,
we hope the Word of God is in our heart.

Memory Verse: Please study and memorize.
Matthew: 12:50
"For whoever does the will of my heavenly Father, is my brother, and sister, and mother."

QUESTIONS and RESPONSES

1. What did Jesus do on the Sabbath?

2. Why did Jesus do this on the Sabbath?

3. What does a good person bring forth?

4. What will happen on the day of our judgment?

5. Compare Exodus 34:21 in the Old Testament to Matthew 12:1-2 in the New Testament.

6. What was an important message in this chapter?

7. After reading and reflecting on this chapter, what do I want to thank God for?

***If the Word of God is in our mind,
we hope the Word of God is in our heart.***

Memory Verse: Please study and memorize.
Matthew: 13:9 and 13:43
"Whoever has ears ought to hear."

QUESTIONS and RESPONSES

1. Name three parables.

2. What is the purpose of parables?

3. What is the message in the parable of the sower?

4. What is the message in the parable of the mustard seed?

5. Compare Matthew 13:35 in the New Testament to Psalm 78:2 in the Old Testament.

6. What was an important message in this chapter?

7. After reading and reflecting on this chapter, what do I want to thank God for?

If the Word of God is in our mind,
we hope the Word of God is in our heart

Memory Verse: Please study and memorize.
Matthew: 14:27b
"Take courage, it is 1; do not be afraid."

QUESTIONS and RESPONSES

1. Who was responsible for the death of John the Baptist?

2. Name two miracles in this chapter.

3. What did the people of Gennesaret beg for?

4. What is the fourth watch of the night?

5. Compare 2 Kings 4:42-44 in the Old Testament to Matthew 14:13-21 in the New Testament.

6. What was an important message in this chapter?

7. After reading and reflecting on this chapter, what do I want to thank God for?

If the Word of God is in our mind, we hope the Word of God is in our heart.

Memory Verse: Please study and memorize.

Matthew: 15:4a

For God said, "Honor your father and your mother."

QUESTIONS and RESPONSES

1. What commandment is stated in this chapter?

2. What woman had great faith?

3. Name at least two healings by Jesus.

4. Why did Jesus want to feed the crowds?

5. What message is in Exodus 20:12 in the Old Testament that is like Matthew 15:4 in the New Testament?

6. What was an important message in this chapter?

7. After reading and reflecting on this chapter, what do I want to thank God for?

If the Word of God is in our mind,
we hope the Word of God is in our heart

Memory Verse: Please study and memorize.

Matthew: 16:18

"And I say to you, you are Peter, and upon this rock I will build my church, and the gates of the netherworld shall not prevail against it."

QUESTIONS and RESPONSES

1. Who were the Pharisees and Sadducees?

2. Who did Jesus give the keys to the kingdom of heaven to?

3. Who said this: "Whoever wishes to come after me must deny himself, take up his cross, and follow me"?

4. Who was this said to: "Whoever wishes to come after me must deny himself, take up his cross, and follow me"?

5. Who is mentioned in Matthew verse 16:14 in the New Testament and also the Old Testament, Malachi 3:23?

6. What was an important message in this chapter?

7. After reading and reflecting on this chapter, what do I want to thank God for?

If the Word of God is in our mind,
we hope the Word of God is in our heart.

Memory Verse: Please study and memorize.
Matthew: 17:20
"If you have faith the size of a mustard seed, you will say to this mountain, 'Move from here to there, and it will move. Nothing will be impossible for you."

QUESTIONS and RESPONSES

1. Describe the Transfiguration of Jesus.

2. What is important for healing to take place?

3. Where did the disciples gather?

4. What did Jesus compare faith to?

5. What does Matthew 17:1 in the New Testament have in it that is like Exodus 24:12 in the Old Testament?

6. What was an important message in this chapter?

7. After reading and reflecting on this chapter, what do I want to thank God for?

If the Word of God is in our mind,
we hope the Word of God is in our heart.

Memory Verse: Please study and memorize.

Matthew: 18:20

"For where two or three are gathered together in my name, there am I in the midst of them."

QUESTIONS and RESPONSES

1. Who is the greatest in the kingdom of heaven?

2. Name two parables in this chapter.

3. What are you to do if your brother sins?

4. If two or three are praying together, who is in their midst?

5. How is Matthew 18:22 in the New Testament like Genesis 4:24 in the Old Testament?

6. What was an important message in this chapter?

7. After reading and reflecting on this chapter, what do I want to thank God for?

If the Word of God is in our mind,
we hope the Word of God is in our heart

Memory Verse: Please study and memorize.

Matthew: 19:30

"But many who are first will be last, and the last will be first."

QUESTIONS and RESPONSES

1. What did Jesus do for the children?

2. What answer did Jesus give when He was asked: "What good must I do to gain eternal life?"

3. (Complete the sentence.) It is easier for a camel to pass through an eye...

4. What will those who have given up house, family and land to follow Jesus receive?

5. What is in the Old Testament Exodus 20:12-16 that is like Matthew 19:18-19 in the New Testament?

6. What was an important message in this chapter?

7. After reading and reflecting on this chapter, what do I want to thank God for?

If the Word of God is in our mind, we hope the Word of God is in our heart.

Memory Verse: Please study and memorize.

Matthew: 20:27

"The Son of Man did not come to be served but to serve and give His life as a ransom for the many."

QUESTIONS and RESPONSES

1. Why did Jesus say: "Are you envious because I am generous?"

2. What prediction was Jesus giving?

3. What did Jesus mean when He said: "He did not come to be served but to serve and to give His life as a ransom for many?"

4. What did Jesus do for the two blind men?

5. Compare the Old Testament of 1 Kings 1:11 to Matthew 20:20 in the New Testament.

6. What was an important message in this chapter?

7. After reading and reflecting on this chapter, what do I want to thank God for?

If the Word of God is in our mind,
we hope the Word of God is in our heart.

Memory Verse: Please study and memorize.
Matthew: 21:22
"Whatever you ask for in prayers with faith, you will receive."

QUESTIONS and RESPONSES

1. Whose entry was made into Jerusalem? Describe it.

2. What was taking place in the Temple?

3. What message did you get from the Parable of the Two Sons?

4. What message did you get from the Parable of the Tenants?

5. How is the verse in the Old Testament of Psalm 8:3 like Matthew 21:16 in the New Testament?

6. What was an important message in this chapter?

7. After reading and reflecting on this chapter, what do I want to thank God for?

If the Word of God is in our mind,
we hope the Word of God is in our heart.

Memory Verse: Please study and memorize.

Matthew: 22:14

"Many are invited, but few are chosen."

QUESTIONS and RESPONSES

1. What is a message from the Parable of the Wedding Feast?

2. Who are the hypocrites in this chapter?

3. At the resurrection of the body from the dead, it will be like....

4. What is the greatest commandment?

5. What similarities are there in the verse from the Old Testament of Daniel 12:2 with Matthew 22:23 in the New Testament?

6. What was an important message in this chapter?

7. After reading and reflecting on this chapter, what do I want to thank God for?

*If the Word of God is in our mind,
we hope the Word of God is in our heart.*

Memory Verse: Please study and memorize.

Matthew: 23:11

"The greatest among you must be your servant."

QUESTIONS and RESPONSES

1. Who are the hypocrites in this chapter?

2. Name two things the hypocrites did?

3. What are the blind to do?

4. What people were murdered?

5. How does Deuteronomy 14:22 in the Old Testament compare with Matthew 23:23 in the New Testament?

6. What was an important message in this chapter?

7. After reading and reflecting on this chapter, what do I want to thank God for?

If the Word of God is in our mind,
we hope the Word of God is in our heart.

Memory Verse: Please study and memorize.

Matthew: 24:44

"So too, you also must be prepared, for at an hour you do not expect, the Son of Man will come."

QUESTIONS and RESPONSES

1. What Mount was Jesus at in this chapter and who was there with Him? Jesus was at the Mount of Olives and the disciples were with Him. Verse 24:3

2. What is the coming of the Son of Man to be like?

3. What is the lesson of the fig tree?

4. What kind of hour will it be when the Son of Man comes?

5. Compare Matthew 24:30 in the New Testament to Zechariah 12:12 in the Old Testament.

6. What was an important message in this chapter?

7. After reading and reflecting on this chapter, what do I want to thank God for?

If the Word of God is in our mind, we hope the Word of God is in our heart.

Memory Verse: Please study and memorize.

Matthew: 25:13

"Therefore, stay awake, for you know neither the day nor the hour."

QUESTIONS and RESPONSES

1. What is the message in the parable of the ten virgins?

2. What is the message in the parable of the talents?

3. What is the message in the story of the Judgment of the Nations?

4. Name two or more things that we should do to gain eternal life' stated in this chapter.

5. Compare Matthew 25:31 in the New Testament to Daniel 7:13 in the Old Testament.

6. What was an important message in this chapter?

7. After reading and reflecting on this chapter, what do I want to thank God for?

If the Word of God is in our mind,
we hope the Word of God is in our heart.

Memory Verse: Please study and memorize.
Matthew: 26:41
"Watch and pray that you may not undergo the test. The spirit is willing, but the flesh is weak."

QUESTIONS and RESPONSES

1. Who betrayed Jesus and how much was be willing to turn Jesus over for?

2. What happened at the Lord's Supper?

3. Who said: "Even though I should have to die with you, I will not deny you." And what happened?

4. What did Jesus do in Gethsemane?

5. Why is the verse in Zechariah 13:7 in the Old Testament like Matthew 26:31 in the New Testament?

6. What was an important message in this chapter?

7. After reading and reflecting on this chapter, what do I want to thank God for?

*If the Word of God is in our mind,
we hope the Word of God is in our heart*

Memory Verse: Please study and memorize.
Matthew: 27:11b
"Are you King of the Jews?"

QUESTIONS and RESPONSES

1. How did Judas die?

2. Who was released instead of Jesus?

3. Who mocked and crucified Jesus?

4. Who were some of the women present at the death of Jesus?

5. Why is the verse in Matthew 27:65 in the New Testament like 2 Kings 2:11 in the Old Testament?

6. What was an important message in this chapter?

7. After reading and reflecting on this chapter, what do I want to thank God for?

If the Word of God is in our mind,
we hope the Word of God is in our heart.

Memory Verse: Please study and memorize.
Matthew: 28:20b
"And behold I am with you always, until the end of the age."

QUESTIONS and RESPONSE

1. Who came to the tomb on the first day after the Sabbath?

2. What did the angel say when they came to the tomb?

3. Where did the eleven disciples go?

4. What did Jesus tell the disciples to go and do?

5. Why is the verse in Daniel 7:14 in the Old Testament like Matthew 28:20 in the New Testament?

6. What was an important message in this chapter?

7. After reading and reflecting on this chapter, what do I want to thank God for?

If the Word of God is in our mind,
it may become closer to our hearts.
MARK

Memory Verse: Mark 1:17
Jesus said to them, "Come after me, and I will make you fishers of men."

QUESTIONS FOR REFLECTION AND RESPONSE:

1. What was an important sacrament in the beginning of Jesus' Ministry? Why?

2. What might we need to leave in order to follow Jesus more faithfully?

3. What are two cures by Jesus and what meaning do they have for me?

4. Where did Jesus often go and for what reason? Do I do this?

5. How is the passage in Numbers 12:10 of the Old Testament like Mark 1:40 of the New Testament?

6. What was an important message in this chapter?

7. After reading and reflecting on this chapter, what do I need to thank God for?

If the Word of God is in our mind,
it may become closer to our hearts.
MARK

Memory Verse: Mark 2:17
Those who are well do not need a physician, but the sick do. I did not come
to call the righteous but sinners.".".

QUESTIONS FOR REFLECTION AND RESPONSE:

1. How did the people feel about the healing of the paralytic?

2. Who did Jesus eat dinner with?

3. How do I handle the question of fasting?

4. How do I handle the question of what is unlawful on the Sabbath?

5. How is Leviticus 24:9 in the Old Testament like Mark 2:25-26 in the New
    Testament?

6. What was an important message in this chapter?

7. After reading and reflecting on this chapter, what do I want to thank God
    for?

If the Word of God is in our mind,
it may become closer to our hearts.
MARK

Memory Verse: Mark 3:35
"For whoever does the will of God is my brother and sister and mother."

QUESTIONS FOR REFLECTION AND RESPONSE:

1. Why did Jesus cure the man with a withered hand on the Sabbath?

2. What is interesting about the Mission of the Twelve?

3. How did Jesus speak to the crowds?

4. Who does Jesus say His family is?

5. How is Matthew 10:1-4 in the New Testament like Mark 2:13-18 in the New Testament?

6. What was an important message in this chapter?

7. After reading on this chapter, what do I want to thank God for?

If the Word of God is in our mind, it may become closer to our hearts.
MARK

Memory Verse: Mark 4:41
They were filled with great awe and said to one another, "Who then is this whom even the wind and sea obey."

QUESTIONS FOR REFLECTION AND RESPONSE:

1. What message do I personally hear from the parable of the sower?

2. What message do I personally hear from the parable of the lamp?

3. What message do I personally hear from the parable of the mustard seed?

4. What message do I personally hear from the passage of the Calming of the Storm?

5. How is the passage from the Old Testament of Ezekiel 17:23 like the passage from Mark 4:32 in the New Testament?

6. What was an important message in this chapter?

7. After reading and reflecting on this chapter what do I want to thank God for?

If the Word of God is in our mind,
it may become closer to our hearts.
MARK

Memory Verse: Mark 5:19
"Go home to your family and announce to them all that the Lord in His pity has done for you."

QUESTIONS FOR REFLECTION AND RESPONSE:

1. What happened to the possessed man? How would I have reacted?

2. What saved the women in this chapter?

3. What cure did I like the best in this chapter? Why?

4. How is Mark 5:39 of the New Testament like Matthew 27:52 of the New Testament?

5. How is Mark 5:39 of the New Testament like John 11:11 of the New Testament?

6. What was an important message in this chapter?

7. After reading and reflecting on this chapter, what do I want to thank God for?

If the Word of God is in our mind,
it may become closer to our hearts.
MARK

Memory Verse: Mark 6:11
"Whatever place does not welcome you or listen to you, leave there and shake the dust off your feet in testimony against them."

QUESTIONS FOR REFLECTION AND RESPONSE:

1. What did the people of Nazareth lack when Jesus was teaching in the synagogues? Why?

2. What did Jesus give the apostles?

3. What insight did I get from the death of John the Baptist?

4. What was fascinating when Jesus and the apostles were working together?

5. How is Isaiah 43:1 of the Old Testament like Mark 6:50 of the New Testament?

6. What was an important message in this chapter?

7. After reading this chapter, what do I want to thank God for?

If the Word of God is in our mind,
it may become closer to our hearts.
MARK

Memory Verse: Mark 7:8
"You disregard God's commandment, but cling to human tradition."

QUESTIONS FOR REFLECTION AND RESPONSE:

1. What was a tradition of the Elders?

2. What did Jesus teach that is important?

3. What was significant about the Syrophoenician woman's faith?

4. What was significant about the healing of the deaf man?

5. How is Matthew 11:5-6 in the New Testament like Mark 7:36 in the New Testament?

6. What was an important message in this chapter?

7. After reading and reflecting on this chapter, what do I want to thank God for?

If the Word of God is in our mind, it may become closer to our hearts.
MARK

Memory Verse: Mark 8:38
"Whoever is ashamed of me and my words in this faithless and sinful genera-
tion, the Son of Man will be ashamed of when he comes in his Father's glory
with the holy angels."

QUESTIONS FOR REFLECTION AND RESPONSE:

1. What are the similarities of Mark 6:34-44 and Mark 8:1-10 in the New
    Testament?

2. Do we ever expect a sign from Heaven like the Pharisees did?

3. What happened at Bethsaida and what significance does this have in my life?

4. What are some conditions for discipleship?

5. How is Numbers 14:11 in the Old Testament like Mark 8:11 in the New
    Testament?

6. What was an important message in this chapter?

7. After reading and reflecting on this chapter, what do I want to thank God for?

If the Word of God is in our mind,
it may become closer to our hearts.
MARK

Memory Verse: Mark 9:37
"Whoever receives one child such as this in my name, receives me; and whoever receives me, receives not me but the One who sent me."

QUESTIONS FOR REFLECTION AND RESPONSE:

1. What message is in the passage on the Transfiguration of Jesus?

2. Why couldn't the disciples drive the demon out of the boy?

3. Who does Jesus say will be the greatest in the kingdom of heaven?

4. What is to happen if we cause one of these little ones to sin?

5. How is Mark 9:9-13 of the New Testament like Malachi 3:23-24 of the Old Testament?

6. What was an important message in this chapter?

7. After reading and reflecting on this chapter, what do I want to thank God for?

If the Word of God is in our mind, it may become closer to our hearts.
MARK

Memory Verse: Mark 10:31
"But many that are first will be last, and the last will be first."

QUESTIONS FOR REFLECTION AND RESPONSE:

1. How do we need to accept the kingdom of God?

2. What must we do to inherit eternal life?

3. What did the Third Prediction include?

4. Why did the Son of Man come?

5. What in the New Testament of Mark 10:23 is similar to Isaiah 3:10 of the Old Testament?

6. What was an important message in this chapter?

7. After reading and reflecting on this chapter, what do I want to thank God for?

If the Word of God is in our mind,
it may become closer to our hearts.
MARK

Memory Verse: Mark 11:25
"When you stand to pray, forgive anyone against whom you have a grievance, so that your heavenly Father may in turn forgive you your transgressions."

QUESTIONS FOR REFLECTION AND RESPONSE:

1. What was the entry into Jerusalem like?

2. What is the Temple to be called?

3. What is a message Jesus gives Peter in regard to the withered fig tree?

4. Who questioned the authority of Jesus?

5. How is the verse in the Old Testament of Hosea 2:14 like the verse in the New Testament of Mark 11:13?

6. What was an important message in this chapter?

7. After reading and reflecting on this chapter, what do I want to thank God for?

If the Word of God is in our mind,
it may become closer to our hearts.
MARK

Memory Verse: Mark 12:24
Jesus said to them, "Are you not mislead because you do not know the scripture or the power of God?"

QUESTIONS FOR REFLECTION AND RESPONSE:

1. What is the message in the parable of the tenants?

2. What is a message in the passage of paying taxes to the emperor?

3. What is the Greatest Commandment?

4. What is a message in the passage of the poor widow's contribution?

5. How is Psalm 110:1 in the Old Testament like Mark 12:36 in the New Testament?

6. What was an important message in this chapter?

7. After reading and reflecting on this chapter, what do I want to thank God for?

If the Word of God is in our mind,
it may become closer to our hearts.
MARK

Memory Verse: Mark 13:13
"You will be hated by all because of my name. But the one who perseveres to the end will be saved."

QUESTIONS FOR REFLECTION AND RESPONSE:

1. What are signs of the end??

2. How will the Son of Man come?

3. What is the lesson of the fig tree?

4. Why do we need to be watchful?

5. How is the passage in the New Testament of Mark 13:26 like the passage in the Old Testament in Exodus 34:5?

6. What was an important message in this chapter?

7. After reading and reflecting on this chapter, what do I want to thank God for?

If the Word of God is in our mind,
it may become closer to our hearts.
MARK

Memory Verse: Mark 14:9
"Amen, I say to you, wherever the gospel is proclaimed to the whole world, what she has done will be told in memory of her."

QUESTIONS FOR REFLECTION AND RESPONSE:

1. What was significant about the woman at Bethany?

2. Who was the betrayer and what did he do?

3. What was significant about the Lord's Supper?

4. What insight did I get from the passage of the Agony in the Garden?

5. How is the passage from the Old Testament of Deuteronomy 16:1-8 like the passage in the New Testament of Mark 14:1?

6. What was an important message in this chapter?

7. After reading and reflecting on this chapter, what do I want to thank God for?

If the Word of God is in our mind,
it may become closer to our hearts.
MARK

Memory Verse: Mark 15:39b
"Truly this was the Son of God!"

QUESTIONS FOR REFLECTION AND RESPONSE:

1.   What was significant for me in the sentence of the death of Jesus?

2.   What was significant for me in the passage of the crucifixion?

3.   What was significant for me in the passage on the actual death of Jesus?

4.   What was significant for me in the passage on the actual burial of Jesus?

5.   How is the verse from the Old Testament of Psalm 22:2 like the verse from the New Testament of Mark 15:34?

6.   What was an important message in this chapter?

7.   After reading and reflecting on this chapter, what do I want to thank God for?

If the Word of God is in our mind, it may become closer to our hearts.
MARK

Memory Verse: Mark 16:15
"Go into the whole world and proclaim the gospel to every creature."

QUESTIONS FOR REFLECTION AND RESPONSE:

1. What insight or verse tells me that Jesus rose from the dead?

2. "If you do not believe, you have a hardness of heart." What could this mean?

3. Matthew 28:1-10, Mark 16:1-8 and Luke 24:1-12 are all about what? How are they alike?

4. What are some differences from the passages from question 3?

5. What was significant to me about the Ascension of Jesus?

6. What was an important message in this chapter?

7. After reading and reflecting on this chapter, what do I want to thank God for?

If the Word of God is on our mind,
hopefully it will be close to our heart

Memory Verse: Please study and memorize.
Luke 1:45: "Blessed are you who believed that what was spoken to you by the Lord would be fulfilled."

QUESTIONS AND RESPONSES

1. What seemed of importance in the passage of the Announcement of the Birth of John?

2. What seemed of importance in the passage of the Announcement of the Birth of Jesus?

3. What is the name of the passage read every evening by clergy, religious and lay people as the prayer of the Church, Luke 1:46-56?

4. What is the name of the passage read every morning by clergy, religious and lay people as the prayer of the Church, Luke 1:67-80?

5. What is the meaning in the verse of Luke 1:69 of the New Testament and is like the verse of Psalm 18:3 in the Old Testament?

6. What was an important message for me in this chapter?

7. After reading and reflecting on this chapter, what do I want to thank God for?

If the Word of God is on our mind, hopefully it will be close to our heart

Memory Verse: Please study and memorize.

Luke 2:14

"Glory to God in the highest and on earth peace to those on whom his favor rests."

QUESTIONS AND RESPONSES

1. What seemed of importance in the passage on the Birth of Jesus?

2. What was the most significant part of the visit of the Shepherds?

3. Why was there a Presentation of Jesus in the Temple?

4. What did Jesus do in the Temple when He was a boy? Why?

5. What is similar between the passage in the Old Testament in Wisdom 7:4-6 and the passage in the New Testament of Luke 2:7?

6. What was an important message for me in this chapter?

7. After reading and reflecting on this chapter, what do I want to thank God for?

If the Word of God is on our mind, hopefully it will be close to our heart

Memory Verse: Please study and memorize.

Luke 3:11

"Whoever has two cloaks should share with the person who has none. And whoever has food should do likewise."

QUESTIONS AND RESPONSES

1. What seemed of importance in the passage on the preaching of John the Baptist?

2. What happened at the Baptism of Jesus?

3. Why was Jesus baptized?

4. What are my thoughts on the Genealogy of Jesus?

5. How is the verse Psalm 2:7 of the Old Testament like Luke 3:22 of the New Testament?

6. What was an important message for me in this chapter?

7. After reading and reflecting on this chapter, what do I want to thank God for?

If the Word of God is on our mind, hopefully it will be close to our heart

Memory Verse: Please study and memorize.

Luke 4:8

"You shall worship the Lord, your God, and Him alone shall you serve."

QUESTIONS AND ANSWERS

1. What seemed of importance in the passage on the Temptation of Jesus?

2. Where did Jesus go to begin His Ministry?

3. What happened at Nazareth when Jesus preached?

4. What were some of the healings or cures in this chapter?

5. How is the verse Deuteronomy 8:2 of the Old Testament like Luke 4:2 of the New Testament?

6. What was an important message for me in this chapter?

7. After reading and reflecting on this chapter, what do I want to thank God for?

If the Word of God is on our mind,
hopefully it will be close to our heart.

Memory Verse: Please study and memorize.

Luke 5:32

"I have not come to call the righteous to repentance but sinners."

QUESTIONS AND RESPONSES

1. What was significant in the passage of the call of Simon Peter, the fisherman?

2. What was the story about when Jesus called Matthew, Levi, the tax collector?

3. What are two cures or healings in this chapter?

4. What was Jesus' teaching concerning fasting in this chapter?

5. How is the verse in the New Testament Luke 5:14 like the verse in Leviticus 14:2 of the Old Testament?

6. What was an important message for me in this chapter?

7. After reading and reflecting on this chapter, what do I want to thank God for?

If the Word of God is on our mind,
hopefully it will be close to our heart.

Memory Verse: Please study and memorize.

Luke 6:12

"In those days He departed to the mountain to pray, and He spent the night in prayer to God."

QUESTIONS AND RESPONSES

1. The Sabbath is a day for rest, but what are two deeds that are more important?

2. How many disciples did Jesus call? Who became a traitor?

3. Why did people want to touch Jesus?

4. What are the differences and similarities of Luke 6:20-26 and Matthew 5:1-12?

5. What does Jesus say about the one who listens and acts and the one who listens and does not act?

6. What was an important message for me in this chapter?

7. After reading and reflecting on this chapter, what do I want to thank God for?

If the Word of God is on our mind,
hopefully it will be close to our heart.

Memory Verse: Please study and memorize.
Luke 7:50b
"Your faith has saved you; go in peace."

QUESTIONS AND RESPONSES

1. Who was ill and about to die? What did Jesus do?

2. Who died? What did Jesus do?

3. What was the most important thing about the sinful woman?

4. What is similar in verse Luke 7:27 in the New Testament and Malachi 3:1 in the Old Testament?

5. Who acknowledged the righteousness of God and who did not?

6. What was an important message for me in this chapter?

7. After reading and reflecting on this chapter, what do I want to thank God for?

If the Word of God is on our mind,
hopefully it will be close to our heart.

Memory Verse: Please study and memorize.

Luke 8:15

"But as for the seed that fell on rich soil, they are the ones who, when they have heard the word, embrace it with a generous and good heart, and bear fruit through perseverance."

QUESTIONS AND RESPONSES

1. What did Jesus do when He went from one town and village to another?

2. What were some parables that Jesus taught with?

3. What were some healings that he did?

4. In the parable of the sower, the seed is the_____.

5. How is the verse Luke 8:31 in the New Testament similar to Genesis 1:2 in the Old Testament?

6. What was an important message for me in this chapter?

7. After reading and reflecting on this chapter, what do I want to thank God for?

If the Word of God is on our mind,
hopefully it will be close to our heart.

Memory Verse: Please study and memorize.

Luke 9:23

"If anyone wishes to come after me, he must deny himself and take up his cross daily and follow me."

QUESTIONS AND RESPONSES

1. What did Jesus give to the twelve?

2. How did Jesus pray in this chapter?

3. What did Jesus say in the First Prediction of the Passion?

4. What did Jesus say in the Second Prediction of the Passion?

5. How is the verse Luke 9:5 like the verse Matthew 10:14 in the New Testament?

6. What was an important message for me in this chapter?

7. After reading and reflecting on this chapter, what do I want to thank God for?

If the Word of God is on our mind,
hopefully it will be close to our heart

Memory Verse: Please study and memorize.

Luke 10:27

"You shall love the Lord, your God, with all your heart, with all your being, with all your strength, and with all your mind, and your neighbor as yourself."

QUESTIONS AND RESPONSES

1. How many did the Lord appoint as followers on a mission?

2. What is the greatest commandment?

3. How are we to treat our neighbor?

4. What quality of Mary did Jesus point out when Martha was anxious with serving?

5. How is the verse Matthew 10:13 like Luke 10:5 in the New Testament?

6. What was an important message for me in this chapter?

7. After reading and reflecting on this chapter, what do I want to thank God for?

If the Word of God is on our mind, hopefully it will be close to our heart

Memory Verse: Please study and memorize.
Luke 11:9
"And I tell you, ask and you will receive; seek and you will find; knock and the door will be opened to you."

QUESTIONS AND RESPONSES

1. What prayer did Jesus teach the disciples?

2. Jesus said: "Ask and you will _____.
    Seek and you will _____.
    Knock and the door will be _____.

3. "Blessed are those who hear the word of God and_____.

4. What did Jesus tell the Pharisees to pay attention to?

5. How is Luke 11:1-4 and Matthew 6:9-13 in the New Testament different and similar?

6. What was an important message for me in this chapter?

7. After reading and reflecting on this chapter, what do I want to thank God for?

If the Word of God is on our mind,
hopefully it will be close to our heart.

Memory Verse: Please study and memorize.
Luke 12:48b
"Much will be required of the person entrusted with much, and still more will be demanded of the person entrusted with more."

QUESTIONS AND RESPONSES

1. What are we to have under persecution?

2. Who will help you teach others about Jesus?

3. What matters are we to be rich in?

4. We are not to worry or be anxious so what are we to seek?

5. How is Luke 12:1 like Mark 8:15 in the New Testament?

6. What was an important message for me in this chapter?

7. After reading and reflecting on this chapter, what do I want to thank God for?

If the Word of God is on our mind,
hopefully it will be close to our heart

Memory Verse: Please study and memorize.

Luke 13:24

"Strive to enter through the narrow gate, for many, I tell you, will attempt to enter but will not be strong enough."

QUESTIONS AND RESPONSES

1. What will happen to those wbo do not repent? What does repent mean?

2. Name at least three parables in this chapter.

3. What is meant by the narrow door?

4. What did Jesus do on the Sabbath? Why was this, a good act?

5. How is Exodus 20:9-10 in the Old Testament like Luke 13:14 in the New Testament?

6. What was an important message for me in this chapter?

7. After reading and reflecting on this chapter, what do I want to thank God for?

If the Word of God is on our mind, hopefully it will be close to our heart

Memory Verse: Please study and memorize.

Luke 14:13

"Rather, when you hold a banquet, invite the poor, the crippled, the lame, the blind."

QUESTIONS AND RESPONSES

1. Who was healed on the Sabbath?

2. Who does Jesus recommend to be the invited guests at a banquet?

3. What was interesting in the parable of the Great Feast?

4. What are some sayings about discipleship?

5. How is Proverbs 25:6 in the Old Testament like Luke 14:8 in the New Testament?

6. What was an important message for me in this chapter?

7. After reading and reflecting on this chapter, what do I want to thank God for?

If the Word of God is on our mind, hopefully it will be close to our heart.

Memory Verse: Please study and memorize.
Luke 15:10
"In just the same way, I tell you, there will be rejoicing among the angels of God over one sinner who repents."

QUESTIONS AND RESPONSES

1. What are the three parables in this chapter?

2. What are we to do when a sinner repents?

3. What did the scribes and Pharisees complain about?

4. What do the parables in this chapter teach us?

5. How is Proverbs 18:24 in the Old Testament like Luke 15:32 in the New Testament?

6. What was an important message for me in this chapter?

7. After reading and reflecting on this chapter, what do I want to thank God for?

If the Word of God is on our mind, hopefully it will be close to our heart

Memory Verse: Please study and memorize.

Luke 16:13

"No servant can serve two masters. He will either hate one and love the other, or be devoted to one and despise the other. You cannot serve God and mammon."

QUESTIONS AND RESPONSES

1. What is a teaching about honesty?

2. What is a saying against the Pharisees in regards to money?

3. Who was the poor man in the parable?

4. Is it bad to be rich?

5. How is Matthew 6:24 in the New Testament like Luke 16:13 in the New Testament?

6. What was an important message for me in this chapter?

7. After reading and reflecting on this chapter, what do I want to thank God for?

If the Word of God is on our mind,
hopefully it will be close to our heart.

Memory Verse: Please study and memorize.
Luke 17:4
"And if he wrongs you seven times in one day and returns to you seven times saying, 'I am sorry,' you should forgive him."

QUESTIONS AND RESPONSES

1. What are you to do if your brother sins?

2. What did the apostles say to the Lord?

3. What did one of the ten lepers that were cleansed do?

4. What did Jesus say to the foreigner who returned to give thanks?

5. How is Genesis 6:8 in the Old Testament like Luke 17:26 in the New Testament?

6. What was an important message for me in this chapter?

7. After reading and reflecting on this chapter, what do I want to thank God for?

If the Word of God is on our mind,
hopefully it will be close to our heart.

Memory Verse: Please study and memorize.
Luke 18:17
"Amen, I say to you, whoever does not accept the kingdom of God like a child will not enter it."

QUESTIONS AND RESPONSES

1. What helped the judge to deliver a just decision?

2. What does it mean to be humble?

3. How did Jesus respond to children?

4. What was it that saved the blind man?

5. How is Exodus 20:12-17 in the Old Testament like Luke 18:20 in the New Testament?

6. What was an important message for me in this chapter?

7. After reading and reflecting on this chapter, what do I want to thank God for?

If the Word of God is on our mind,
hopefully it will be close to our heart.

Memory Verse: Please study and memorize.

Luke 19:10

"For the Son of Man has come to seek and to save what was lost."

QUESTIONS AND RESPONSES

1.   What lesson can we learn from Zacchaeus?

2.   What lesson can we learn from the parable of the ten gold coins?

3.   On what day in the Church year do we celebrate the Entry into Jerusalem?

4.   What kind of house does Jesus expect the temple to be?

5.   How is the verse in Malachi 3:1 of the Old Testament like the verse in Luke 19:38 of the New Testament?

6.   What was an important message for me in this chapter?

7.   After reading and reflecting on this chapter, what do I want to thank God for?

*If the Word of God is on our mind,
hopefully it will be close to our heart.*

Memory Verse: Please study and memorize.
Luke 20:25
"Then repay to Caesar what belongs to Caesar and to God what belongs to
God."

QUESTIONS AND RESPONSES

1. Who questioned the authority of Jesus?

2. What was a lesson from the parable of the tenant farmers?

3. Why was Jesus being asked questions about the taxes to the Emperor?

4. Why was Jesus being asked questions about the Resurrection?

5. How is Psalm 110:1 in the Old Testament like Luke 20:42-43 in the New
   Testament?

6. What was an important message for me in this chapter?

7. After reading and reflecting on this chapter, what do I want to thank God
   for?

If the Word of God is on our mind,
hopefully it will be close to our heart.

Memory Verse: Please study and memorize.
Luke 21:19
"By your perseverance you will secure your lives."

QUESTIONS AND RESPONSES

1. Why was the widow's contribution so great?

2. What did you find interesting about the end times?

3. What does persecution mean?

4. What will help us to escape tribulations?

5. How is 2 Chronicles 15:6 in the Old Testament like Luke 21:10 in the New Testament?

6. What was an important message for me in this chapter?

7. After reading and reflecting on this chapter, what do I want to thank God for?

*If the Word of God is on our mind,
hopefully it will be close to our heart.*

Memory Verse: Please study and memorize.

Luke 22:46

"Why are you sleeping? Get up and pray that you may not undergo the test."

QUESTIONS AND RESPONSES

1. When was the institution of the Eucharist?

2. What was Peter's denial about?

3. What was the Agony in the Garden about?

4. What was the Betrayal and Arrest of Jesus about?

5. How is Zechariah 9:11 in the Old Testament like Luke 22:20 in the New Testament?

6. What was an important message for me in this chapter?

7. After reading and reflecting on this chapter, what do I want to thank God for?

If the Word of God is on our mind,
hopefully it will be close to our heart.

Memory Verse: Please study and memorize.

Luke 23:43

"Amen, I say to you, today you will be with me in Paradise."

QUESTIONS AND RESPONSES

1. What did Pilate tell the chief priests and the crowds at first?

2. Who did Pilate become friends with?

3. What did the crowds keep yelling at Pilate?

4. When Jesus was crucified, who was on His right and His left?

5. How is Psalm 22:19 in the Old Testament like Luke 23:34 in the New Testament?

6. What was an important message for me in this chapter?

7. After reading and reflecting on this chapter, what do I want to thank God for?

If the Word of God is on our mind,
hopefully it will be close to our heart.

Memory Verse: Please study and memorize.

Luke 24:53

"And they were continually in the temple praising God."

QUESTIONS AND RESPONSES

1. How many days after the crucifixion did Jesus rise from the dead? Who was at the tomb to find this out?

2. What happened on the Road to Emmaus?

3. What happened when Jesus appeared to the disciples after His Resurrection?

4. What was the Ascension like?

5. How is Isaiah 53:3 in the Old Testament like Luke 24:26 in the New Testament?

6. What was an important message for me in this chapter?

7. After reading and reflecting on this chapter, what do I want to thank God for?

The Word of God is BEYOND AWESOME!

Verse of the Chapter: John 1:1
"In the beginning was the Word, and the Word was with God, and the Word was God."

QUESTIONS AND RESPONSES

1. The Gospel of John contains a lot of wondrous deeds. These are also called, what?

2. Who was one of the first people to give testimony of Jesus?

3. In what location was John the Baptist baptizing?

4. The Holy Spirit is often said to come down like a _____ what does this mean?

5. Who were three of the first disciples of Jesus?

6. What symbol is there for "under the fig tree"? How is Micah 4:4 like John 1:48?

7. Write a note of two sentences or more, to Jesus, sharing with Him your FAITH.

The Word of God is BEYOND AWESOME!

Verse of the Chapter: John 2:23
"While he was in Jerusalem for the feast of the Passover, many began to believe in his name when they saw the signs he was doing."

QUESTIONS AND RESPONSES

1. What was the first sign at the beginning of the ministry of Jesus?

2. Who were the people present at the beginning of the ministry of Jesus?

3. Where did this event take place?

4. What event took place that brought sigaificance to the Resurrection?

5. Who was present at this event and what animals were present?

6. How is Hosea 6:2 in the Old Testament like John 2:19 in the New Testament?

7. Write a note of two sentences or more, to Jesus, sharing with Him your HOPE.

The Word of God is BEYOND AWESOME!

Verse of the Chapter: John 3:16
"For God so loved the world that he gave his only Son, so that everyone who believes in him might not perish but might have eternal life."

QUESTIONS AND RESPONSES

1. Who was Nicodemus?

2. What did God give because of his love for the world?

3. What was the purpose of Jesus?

4. What are we to do to have eternal life?

5. Who hates the light?

6. Who comes to the light?

7. Write a note of two sentences or more, to Jesus, sharing with Him your LOVE.

The Word of God is BEYOND AWESOME!

Verse of the Chapter: John 4:34
Jesus said to them, "My food is to do the will of the one who sent me and to finish his work."

QUESTIONS AND RESPONSES

1. Who did Jesus talk to on his way from Judea to Galilee and what did they talk about?

2. What place was this and who's land was nearby?

3. How are people to worship?

4. How long did Jesus stay in Samaria? Why?

5. What was the second sign that Jesus performed in Galilee?

6. How is Deuteronomy 18:15 in the Old Testament like John 4:25 in the New Testament?

7. Write a note of two sentences or more, to Jesus, sharing with Him your FAITH.

The Word of God is BEYOND AWESOME!

Verse of the Chapter: John 5:47
"But if you do not believe his writings how will you believe my words?"

QUESTIONS AND RESPONSES

1. What was the cure on the Sabbath and where did it take place?

2. Why did the Jews try to kill Jesus?

3. Who has eternal life?

4. What justifies Jesus doing what his father does?

5. Whose testimony is greater than John's?

6. How is 1 Samuel 2:6 in the Old Testament like John 5:21 in the New Testament?

7. Write a note of two sentences or more, to Jesus, sharing with Him your HOPE, (at least three minutes)

The Word of God is BEYOND AWESOME!

Verse of the Chapter: John 6:27
"Do not work for food that perishes but for the food that endures for eternal life, which the Son of Man will give you."

QUESTIONS AND RESPONSES

1. Why did the large crowd follow Jesus when He went across the Sea of Galilee?

2. Why did the disciples become afraid when they were in the boat and had rowed out about three or four miles on the sea to Capernaum?

3. Who will not reject anyone who comes to Him?

4. What is the spirit of life?

5. Who betrayed Jesus? Whose son was he?

6. How is the verse Psalm 78:24 in the Old Testament like the verse John 6:31 in the New Testament?

7. Write a note of two sentences or more, to Jesus, sharing with Him your LOVE.

The Word of God is BEYOND AWESOME!

Verse of the Chapter: John 7:24
"Stop judging by appearances, but judge justly."

QUESTIONS AND RESPONSES

1. Why did Jesus just move around within Galilee rather than travel to Judea?

2. Who are the people that are truthful?

3. Who sent guards to arrest Jesus?

4. What is meant by living water?

5. What was the discussion on concerning where the Messiah would come from?

6. How is the verse Exodus 17:6 in the Old Testament like the verse John 7:38 in the New Testament?

7. Write a note of two sentences or more, to Jesus, sharing with Him your FAITH.

The Word of God is BEYOND AWESOME!

Verse of the Chapter: John 8:34
"Amen, amen, I say to you, everyone who commits sin is a slave of sin."

QUESTIONS AND RESPONSES

1. What was Jesus doing in the temple area in the morning?

2. What will people have if they follow Jesus?

3. What did Jesus tell the Jews about how they would be if they believed in Him?

4. Who were the people who asked Jesus if He was possessed?

5. What did Jesus do when they picked up stones to throw at Him?

6. How is the verse of John 8:7 in the New Testament like Deuteronomy 17:7 in the Old Testament?

7. Write a note of two sentences or more, to Jesus, sharing with Him your HOPE.

The Word of God is BEYOND AWESOME!

Verse of the Chapter: John 9:4a
"We have to do the works of the one who sent me while it is still day."

QUESTIONS AND RESPONSE

1.   What was Jesus response when the disciples asked Him who sinned when they saw a blind man, the blind man or his parents?

2.   What was the response of the blind man when others asked him how his eyes were opened?

3.   What was the response of the blind man when the Pharisees asked him, "What do you have to say about him, since he opened your eyes?"

4.   What answer did the parents give when asked the question by the Jews, "How does your son see now?"

5.   What was one of the rules of Jewish Tradition that the Pharisees said Jesus had broken?

6.   How is the verse Exodus 20:5 in the Old Testament like the verse in the New Testament John 9:2?

7.   Write a note of two sentences or more, to Jesus, sharing with Him your LOVE.

The Word of God is BEYOND AWESOME!

Verse of the Chapter: John 10:30
"The Father and I are one."

QUESTIONS AND RESPONSES

1. Why did Jesus come?

2. What does a good shepherd do?

3. What does a good shepherd know?

4. What was the Feast of Dedication?

5. What did Jesus tell the Jews to believe, if they did not believe in Him?

6. How is the verse Psalm 80:2 in the Old Testament like John 10:2 in the New Testament?

7. Write a note of two sentences or more, to Jesus, sharing with Him your FAITH.

The Word of God is BEYOND AWESOME!

Verse of the Chapter: John 11:25
"I am the resurrection and the life; whoever believes in me, even if he dies, will live."

QUESTIONS AND RESPONSES

1. What did Jesus do for Martha and Mary and the crowd?

2. Why did Jesus perform this miracle?

3. Who came to believe in Jesus because of this miracle?

4. What kind of plan did the Pharisees begin to make?

5. Where did Jesus go and who was He with?

6. How are the verses Exodus 19:10-11 in the Old Testament like John 11:55 in the New Testament?

7. Write a note of two sentences or more, to Jesus, sharing with Him your HOPE.

The Word of God is BEYOND AWESOME!

Verse of the Chapter: John 12:36
"While you have the light, believe in the light, so that you may become children of the light."

QUESTIONS AND RESPONSES

1. Why did a large crowd of Jews and the chief priests come to Bethany where Lazarus was?

2. Why were palm branches used to welcome Jesus?

3. What feast were the people gathering for?

4. Who is the ruler of the world that will be driven out?

5. If we believe in Jesus, who must we also believe in?

6. How is the verse 1 Maccabees 13:51 in the Old Testament like John 12:13 in the New Testament?

7. Write a note of two sentences or more, to Jesus, sharing with Him your LOVE.

The Word of God is BEYOND AWESOME!

Verse of the Chapter: John 13:35
"This is how all will know that you are my disciples, if you have love for one another."

QUESTIONS AND RESPONSES

1. When Jesus washed the feet of the disciples, what was He teaching us?

2. When and why was Jesus deeply troubled?

3. What was the new commandment that Jesus gave to us?

4. Who would deny Jesus three times?

5. What was the sign or signal that someone had denied Jesus three times?

6. How is the verse Leviticus 19:18 in the Old Testament like John 13:34 in the New Testament?

7. Write a note of two sentences or more, to Jesus, sharing with Him your FAITH.

The Word of God is BEYOND AWESOME!

Verse of the Chapter: John 14:14
"If you ask anything of me in my name, I will do it."

QUESTIONS AND RESPONSES

1. What will the believers of Jesus do?

2. Who are we to have faith in?

3. If we love Jesus and keep His commandments, what will the Father give us to be with us always?

4. How are we to come to the Father?

5. If Jesus says our hearts are not to be troubled or afraid, then what are they to be?

6. How is the verse Wisdom 6:18 in the Old Testament like John 14:15 in the New Testament?

7. Write a note of two sentences or more, to Jesus, sharing with Him your HOPE.

The Word of God is BEYOND AWESOME!

Verse of the Chapter; John 15:9
"As the Father loves me, so I also love you, Remain in my love."

QUESTIONS AND RESPONSES

1. Who is the vine and who is the vine grower?

2. How can we bear fruit?

3. Why were we given the command to love one another?

4. Who is our Advocate?

5. Who was hated by the world first?

6. How is verse Psalm 69:5 in the Old Testament like John 15:25 in the New Testament?

7. Write a note of two sentences or more, to Jesus, sharing with Him your LOVE.

The Word of God is BEYOND AWESOME!

Verse of the Chapter: John 16:33
"I have told you this so that you might have peace in me. In the world you have trouble, but take courage, I have conquered the world."

QUESTIONS AND RESPONSES

1. Who will guide us to all truth?

2. Why are we to ask the Father for things in Jesus' name?

3. When we have trouble in this world, why are we to have courage?

4. How has the ruler of the world been condemned?

5. Who realized that they did not need to question Jesus anymore?

6. How is the verse Jeremiah 31:13 in the Old Testament like John 16:20 in the New Testament?

7. Write a note of two sentences or more, to Jesus, sharing with Him your FAITH.

The Word of God is BEYOND AWESOME!

Verse of the Chapter: John 17:17
"Consecrate them in truth. Your word is truth."

QUESTIONS AND RESPONSE

1. What was Jesus doing when he raised His eyes to heaven and spoke?

2. What did the messages in this chapter sound like to you? What lesson or meaning did you get?

3. What kind of things did Jesus ask the Father for?

4. What does Jesus wish for us?

5. What does Jesus make known to us from the Father?

6. How is the verse Wisdom 15:3 in the Old Testament like John 17:26 in the New Testament?

7. Write a note of two sentences or more, to Jesus, sharing with Him your HOPE.

The Word of God is BEYOND AWESOME!

Verse of the Chapter: John 18:37b
"Everyone who belongs to the truth listens to my voice."

QUESTIONS AND RESPONSES

1. What may have been symbolic of the hour of darkness?

2. Who asked Peter if he was one of Jesus' disciples?

3. Who questioned Jesus about his disciples and doctrine?

4. What questions did Pilate ask Jesus?

5. What was the custom at Passover?

6. What is in verse 2 Samuel 15:23 of the Old Testament that is like John 18:12 of the New Testament?

7. Write a note of two sentences or more, to Jesus, sharing with Him your LOVE.

The Word of God is BEYOND AWESOME!

Verse of the Chapter: John 19:35
"An eyewitness has testified, and his testimony is true; he knows that he is speaking the truth, so that you also may believe."

QUESTIONS AND RESPONSES

1. What did Pilate have the soldiers do?

2. What did the chief priests and guards cry out when they saw Jesus?

3. Where and with whom was Jesus crucified?

4. What did the inscription say that was written on the cross?

5. Why were the bodies not to remain on the cross?

6. How is the verse Psalm 22:19 in the Old Testament like John 19:24 in the New Testament?

7. Write a note of two sentences or more, to Jesus, sharing with Him your FAITH.

The Word of God is BEYOND AWESOME!

Verse of the Chapter: John 20:21
"Peace be with you. As the Father has sent me, so I send you."

QUESTIONS AND RESPONSES

1. When did Mary and Magdala go to the tomb?

2. What did Jesus tell Mary when she was weeping at the tomb?

3. Where and when did Jesus appear to his disciples? What did He say to them?

4. What disciple was not there when Jesus appeared? What did Jesus say to him when he appeared again?

5. What has been written so that we might come to believe?

6. How is the verse Psalm 22:17 in the Old Testament like John 20:20 in the New Testament?

7. Write a note of two sentences or more, to Jesus, sharing with Him your HOPE.

The Word of God is BEYOND AWESOME!

Verse of the Chapter: John 21:19b
"Follow me."

QUESTIONS AND RESPONSES

1. Where and to what seven disciples did Jesus reveal Himself?

2. What happened when Jesus told the children to cast the net over the right side of the boat?

3. What did Peter and Jesus discuss?

4. What do the words "until I come" mean?

5. Why could one not describe all the things Jesus did?

6. How is the verse Ezekial 47:10 in the Old Testament like John 21:11 in the New Testament?

7. Write a note of two sentences or more, to Jesus, sharing with Him your LOVE.

The Word of God is BEYOND AWESOME!

Verse of the Chapter: Acts of the Apostles 1:14a
"All these devoted themselves with one accord in prayer."

QUESTIONS AND RESPONSES

1. How are we baptized? How did John baptize?

2. What do we call: Jesus being taken up to heaven?

3. Who devoted themselves with one accord in prayer?

4. Who was chosen to take the place of Judas?

5. What was an important thing that the disciples did when selecting Judas' replacement?

6. How is Deuteronomy 8:2 in the Old Testament like Acts of the Apostles 1:3 in the New Testament?

7. Write a note to God, the Father, about your needs and your wants...

The Word of God is BEYOND AWESOME!

Verse of the Chapter: Acts of the Apostles 2:42
"They devoted themselves to the teaching of the apostles and to the communal life, to the breaking of the bread and to the prayers."

QUESTIONS AND RESPONSES

1. What was it like when the time for Pentecost was fulfilled?

2. Who were the people staying in Jerusalem at this time?

3. Why were those people confused?

4. What did Peter tell the Israelites to do?

5. What did the apostles devote themselves to everyday?

6. How is Exodus 19:18 of the Old Testament like Acts of the Apostles 2:3 in the New Testament?

7. Write a note to Jesus sharing your friendship you have with Him now and what you would like it to be like in the future?

The Word of God is BEYOND AWESOME!

Verse of the Chapter: Acts of the Apostles 3:23
"Everyone who does not listen to that prophet will be cut off from the people."

QUESTIONS AND RESPONSES

1. What time did Peter and John go to the temple area to pray?

2. What did Peter do for the crippled beggar?

3. What were the first things the crippled man did after their encounter?

4. Who is called the "author of life"?

5. What was it that the crippled beggar had that made him perfect?

6. How is Deuteronomy 18:15 in the Old Testament like Acts of the Apostles 3:22 in the New Testament?

7. Write a note to the Holy Spirit asking for guidance for every moment of your life?

The Word of God is BEYOND AWESOME!

Verse of the Chapter: Acts of the Apostles 4:31
"As they prayed, the place where they were gathered shook, and they were all filled with the Holy Spirit and continued the word of God with boldness."

QUESTIONS AND RESPONSES

1. What happened to those who came to hear the Word?

2. Who is the stone that was rejected?

3. How was Peter and John described?

4. How did the chief priests and elders pray?

5. What was life like in the Christian Community?

6. How is Exodus 19:18 of the Old Testament like Acts of the Apostles 4:31 in the New Testament?

7. Write a note to God, the Father, about your needs and your wants...

The Word of God is BEYOND AWESOME!

Verse of the Chapter: Acts of the Apostles 5:42
"And all day long, both at the temple and in their homes, they did not stop teaching and proclaiming the Messiah, Jesus."

QUESTIONS AND RESPONSES

1. What was the sin of Ananias and Sapphira?

2. What were some of the signs and wonders performed by the apostles?

3. What did the high priests and Sadducees do to the apostles? Why?

4. What happened to the apostles during the night?

5. A Pharisee in the Sanhedrin, Gamaliel, gave what advice to the Israelites?

6. How is Deuteronomy 13:5 in the Old Testament like Acts of the Apostles 5:29 in the New Testament?

7. Write a note to Jesus sharing your friendship you have with Him now and what you would like it to be like in the future.

The Word of God is BEYOND AWESOME!

Verse of the Chapter: Acts of the Apostles 6:2b
"It is not right for us to neglect the word of God to serve at table. *

QUESTIONS AND RESPONSES

1. What were seven men to be devoted to?

2. What is another name for those seven assistants?

3. Who was working great wonders and signs among the people?

4. What was the essential function of the twelve apostles?

5. What is the customary Jewish way of designating persons for a task and invoking upon them the divine blessing and power to perform it?

6. How is Exodus 20:21 in the Old Testament like the verse in the New Testament Acts of the Apostles 6:14?

7. Write a note to the Holy Spirit and ask for the wisdom to make good choices.

The Word of God is BEYOND AWESOME!

Verse of the Chapter: Acts of the Apostles 7:55
"But he, filled with the Holy Spirit, looked up intently to heaven and saw the glory of God and Jesus standing at the right hand of God."

QUESTIONS AND RESPONSES

1. Who sold Joseph into slavery in Egypt?

2. How was Moses educated?

3. Where and how did an angel appear to Moses?

4. What happened to Stephen?

5. What were the last words of Stephen?

6. How is Exodus 1:5 in the Old Testament like Acts of the Apostles 7:9 in the New Testament?

7. Write a note to God, the Father, about your needs and your wants...

The Word of God is BEYOND AWESOME!

Verse of the Chapter: Acts of the Apostles 8:22
"Repent of this wickedness of yours and pray to the lord that, if possible, your intention may be forgiven."

QUESTIONS AND RESPONSES

1. Where was the persecution of the church taking place?

2. What were some of the signs performed by Phillip?

3. What did Simon do before he was baptized by Phillip?

4. The angel of the Lord spoke to Phillip and where was he told to go?

5. Why did Phillip and the eunuch go down into the water?

6. How is Isaiah 53:7 in the Old Testament like Acts of the Apostle 8:32 in the New Testament?

7. Write a note to Jesus sharing your friendship you have with Him now and what you would like it to be like in the future.

The Word of God is BEYOND AWESOME!

Verse of the Chapter: Acts of the Apostles 9:20
"and he began at once to proclaim Jesus in the synagogues, that He is the Son of God."

QUESTIONS AND RESPONSES

1. What happened to Saul on his way to Damascus?

2. What did the disciple, Ananias do for Saul?

3. What happened to Saul in Jerusalem?

4. In what countries was the church at peace?

5. Who did Peter heal?

6. How is Psalm 2:7 in the Old Testament like Acts of the Apostle 9:20 in the New Testament?

7. Write a note to the Holy Spirit and ask for the wisdom to make good choices.

The Word of God is BEYOND AWESOME!

Verse of the Chapter: Acts of the Apostles 10:44
"While Peter was still speaking these things, the holy Spirit fell upon all who were listening to the word."

QUESTIONS AND RESPONSES

1. What was the vision of Cornelius?

2. What was the vision of Peter?

3. In the Bible, what was often used as a number of days?

4. What time in the afternoon did a lot of things happen in the New Testament?

5. Who said: "In truth, I see that God shows no partiality"?

6. How is Wisdom 6:7 in the Old Testament like Acts of the Apostles 10:34 in the New Testament?

7. Write a note to God, the Father, about your needs and your wants...

The Word of God is BEYOND AWESOME!

Verse of the Chapter: Acts of the Apostles 11:16b
"John baptized with water but you will be baptized with the Holy Spirit."

QUESTIONS AND RESPONSES

1. What group came to accept the word of God and be baptized?

2. Where were the first disciples called Christians?

3. Who were the two disciples that taught a large number of people and met for a whole year?

4. Who was the prophet from Jerusalem who predicted a severe famine?

5. In the Jewish community certain people were referred to as elders or?

6. How is James 5:14 in the New Testament like Acts of the Apostles 11:30 in the New Testament?

7. Write a note to Jesus sharing your friendship you have with Him now and what you would like it to be like in the future.

The Word of God is BEYOND AWESOME!

Verse of the Chapter: Acts of the Apostles 12:24 "But the Word of God continued to spread and grow."

QUESTIONS AND RESPONSES

1. What did Herod do on the Feast of the Unleavened Bread?

2. What did the angel do for Peter when he was in prison?

3. What was happening at the house of Mary, the mother of John?

4. What did Herod do when he found Peter missing from prison?

5. What was the death of Herod like?

6. How is 2 Kings 19:35 in the Old Testament like Acts of the Apostles 12:23 in the New Testament?

7. Write a note to the Holy Spirit and ask for the wisdom to make good choices.

The Word of God is BEYOND AWESOME!

Verse of the Chapter: Acts of the Apostles 13:3
"Then, completing their fasting and prayer, they laid hands on them and sent them off,"

QUESTIONS AND RESPONSES

1.   What happened on the first mission of Saul and Barnabas in Cyprus?

2.   What happened at the synagogue in Antioch?

3.   Who are two of the prophets that Paul was talking about?

4.   Who were some of the people that followed Paul and Barnabas?

5.   What did some of the Jews do when Paul and Barnabas spoke the word of God to the Gentiles?

6.   How is Exodus 12:41 in the Old Testament like Acts of the Apostles 13:20 in the New Testament?

7.   Write a note to God, the Father, about your needs and your wants...

The Word of God is BEYOND AWESOME!

Verse of the Chapter: Acts of the Apostles 14:22b
"It is necessary for us to undergo many hardships to enter the kingdom of God."

QUESTIONS AND RESPONSES

1. What happened at Iconium at the Jewish synagogue when Paul and Barnabas were there?

2. Who told the crowds to turn from worshipping idols to the living God who made heaven and earth and sea and all that is in them?

3. Who healed the crippled man at Lystra?

4. Paul and Barnabas continued to proclaim the good news. They told their disciples to _____ in _____

5. How did they appoint the presbyters in each church?

6. How is Psalm 146:6 in the Old Testament like Acts of the Apostles 15:14b in the New Testament?

7. Write a note to Jesus sharing your friendship you have with Him now and what you would like it to be like in the future.

The Word of God is BEYOND AWESOME!

Verse of the Chapter: Acts of the Apostles 15:8
"And God, who knows the heart, bore witness by granting them the Holy Spirit just as he did us."

QUESTIONS AND RESPONSES

1. What was the journey of Paul and Barnabas through Phoenicia and Samaria to tell all the brothers about? What was the great news of great joy?

2. What are some of the dietary laws stated by James?

3. What was the message in the letter of the apostles delivered by Judas and Silas?

4. What were Paul and Barnabas doing as they remained in Antioch?

5. When Paul and Barnabas separated, who did they each take with them?

6. How is Leviticus 3:17 in the Old Testament like Acts 15:20 in the New Testament?

7. Write a note to the Holy Spirit and ask for the wisdom to make good choices.

The Word of God is BEYOND AWESOME!

Verse of the Chapter: Acts of the Apostles 16:13

"On the Sabbath we went outside the city gate along the river where we thought there would be a place of prayer. We sat and spoke with the women who had gathered there."

QUESTIONS AND RESPONSES

1. Who had a Jewish mother that was a believer and a Greek father?

2. Where were Paul and Silas not to preach?

3. In his vision, Paul was to go where to preach?

4. Who became a believer and paid attention to what Paul was saying? What did she do in response?

5. What happened about midnight when Paul and Silas were praying and singing hymns to God and the prisoners were listening?

6. How is Acts of the Apostles 16:37 like Acts of the Apostles 22:25 in the New Testament?

7. Write a note to God, the Father, about your needs and your wants...

The Word of God is BEYOND AWESOME!

Verse of the Chapter: Acts of the Apostles 17:32
"When they heard about the resurrection of the dead, some began to scoff, but others said, "We should like to hear you on this some other time.""

QUESTIONS AND RESPONSES

1. What did the Jews do that became jealous of Paul and Silas who were discussing the scriptures in Thessalonica?

2. Where did Paul and Silas go during the night? What did they do at this place?

3. Paul was sent ahead to Athens. What did he find happening there?

4. Paul then went to Areopagus. What did he find happening there?

5. Why are we not to think of God as an image fashioned from gold or silver or stone by the human art of imagination?

6. How is Genesis 1:1 in the Old Testament like Acts of the Apostles 17:24 in the New Testament?

7. Write a note to Jesus sharing your friendship you have with Him now and what you would like it to be like in the future.

The Word of God is BEYOND AWESOME!

Verse of the Chapter: Acts of the Apostles 18:4
"Every Sabbath, he entered into discussions in the synagogue, attempting to convince both Jews and Greeks."

QUESTIONS AND RESPONSES

1. What did the Lord say to Paul one night in a vision when he was in Corinth?

2. What did the Jews in Achaia do to Paul and what did they say about him?

3. Where did Paul sail to next and who went along, too?

4. Where did Paul go next and what did he do there?

5. Who was Apollos, the Jew, and what did he do?

6. How is Numbers 6:18 in the Old Testament like Acts of the Apostles 18:18 in the New Testament?

7. Write a note to the Holy Spirit and ask for the wisdom to make good choices.

The Word of God is BEYOND AWESOME!

Verse of the Chapter: Acts of the Apostles 19:20
"Thus did the word of the Lord continue to spread with influence and power."

QUESTIONS AND RESPONSES

1. What happened when Paul was in Ephesus when he first arrived?

2. What happened as a result of the mighty deeds God accomplished at the hands of Paul?

3. What practices did some of the Jews and Greeks in Ephesus have before they became believers?

4. Who were the two people assisting Paul that he sent to Macedonia?

5. Who was known as the great goddess of Asia? Do we believe in this goddess? Why?

6. How is Acts of the Apostles 8:16 in the New Testament like Acts of the Apostles 19:5 in the New Testament?

7. Write a note to God, the Father, about your needs and your wants...

The Word of God is BEYOND AWESOME!

Verse of the Chapter: Acts of the Apostles 20:35b
"It is more blessed to give than to receive."

QUESTIONS AND RESPONSES

1. How long did Paul stay in Greece? Why did he leave?

2. Why did Paul restore Eutychus to life?

3. Where was Paul in a hurry to go and for what day?

4. What was the great desire of Paul to finisb?

5. What did Paul do when he finished speaking?

6. How is 1 Kings 17:21 in the Old Testament like Acts of Apostles 20:10 in the New Testament?

7. Write a note to Jesus sharing your friendship you have with Him now and what you would like it to be like in the future.

The Word of God is BEYOND AWESOME!

Verse of the Chapter: Acts of the Apostles 21:14
"Since he would not be dissuaded we let the matter rest, saying, "The Lord's will be done.""

QUESTIONS AND RESPONSES

1. When Paul left Tyre what did everyone do including the women and children?

2. Where did Paul go when he arrived at Caesarea?

3. Where did Paul go when he arrived in Jerusalem?

4. What did the Jews from Asia do to Paul?

5. After Paul received permission to speak to the people, what language did he speak to them in?

6. How is Numbers 6:5 in the Old Testament like Acts of the Apostles 21:23 in the New Testament?

7. Write a note to the Holy Spirit and ask for the wisdom to make good choices.

The Word of God is BEYOND AWESOME!

Verse of the Chapter: Acts of the Apostles 22:1
"My brothers and fathers, listen to what I am about to say to you in my defense."

QUESTIONS AND RESPONSES

1. What were some of the things Paul told the Jews in Jerusalem about himself?

2. Where was Paul led after he was blinded by the light of Jesus?

3. After Ananias told Paul to regain his sight, what did Paul tell the Jews to do?

4. What kept Paul from being whipped and put in prison?

5. Who freed Paul?

6. How is Luke 24:48 in the New Testament like Acts of the Apostles 22:15 in the New Testament?

7. Write a note to God, the Father, about your needs and your wants...

The Word of God is BEYOND AWESOME!

Verse of the Chapter: Acts of the Apostles 23:11
"The following night the Lord stood by him and said, "Take courage, For just as you have borne witness to my cause in Jerusalem, so you must also bear witness in Rome.""

QUESTIONS AND RESPONSES

1. What was the topic of what the Pharisees and Sadducees were disputing?

2. What was the plot that the Jews made concerning Paul?

3. What information about Paul was secretly given to the commander?

4. What were the soldiers commanded to do?

5. What did the letter to the governor contain that was important information about Paul?

6. How is Exodus 22:27b in the Old Testament like Acts of the Apostles 23:5b in the New Testament?

7. Write a note to Jesus sharing your friendship you have with Him now and what you would like it to be like in the future.

The Word of God is BEYOND AWESOME!

Verse of the Chapter: Acts of the Apostles 24:16
"Because of this, I always strive to keep my conscience clear before God and man."

QUESTIONS AND RESPONSES

1. Who were the Nazoreans?

2. What did Paul tell the governor in his defense?

3. What did Paul say that he was on trial for?

4. Who left Paul in prison?

5. Who succeeded Felix in Caesarea?

6. How is Luke 23:2 in the New Testament like Acts of the Apostles 24:5 in the New Testament?

7. Write a note to the Holy Spirit and ask for the wisdom to make good choices.

The Word of God is BEYOND AWESOME!

Verse of the Chapter: Acts of the Apostles 25:27
"For it seems senseless to me to send up a prisoner without indicating the charges against him."

QUESTIONS AND RESPONSES

1. Where did the chief priests and Jewish leaders present Festus their formal charges against Paul?

2. What did Paul say in defense of himself?

3. Paul appealed to whom?

4. What did Festus tell King Agrippa and others present about Paul?

5. What seemed senseless to Festus?

6. How is Romans 15:25 in the New Testament like Acts of the Apostles 25:3 in the New Testament?

7. Write a note to God, the Father, about your needs and your wants...

The Word of God is BEYOND AWESOME!

Verse of the Chapter: Acts of the Apostles 26:22
"But I have enjoyed God's help to this very day, and so I stand here testifying to small and great alike, saying nothing different from what the prophets and Moses foretold."

QUESTIONS AND RESPONSES

1. What did Paul have to say to King Agrippa?

2. What happened as Paul was traveling on the road to Damascus?

3. What did the Lord say he appointed Paul to do?

4. Festus told Paul that he was mad and what was Paul's response?

5. What did the king, governor, Bernice and others say to one another about Paul's response?

6. How is Ezekiel 2:1 in the Old Testament like Acts of the Apostles 26:16 in the New Testament?

7. Write a note to Jesus sharing your friendship you have with Him now and what you would like it to be like in the future.

The Word of God is BEYOND AWESOME!

Verse of the Chapter: Acts of the Apostles 27:25
"Therefore, keep up your courage, men; I trust in God that it will turn out as I have been told."

QUESTIONS AND RESPONSES

1. Where did Paul and some other prisoners decide to sail to?

2. What were some of the difficulties as they sailed to Rome?

3. What advice did Paul give to them?

4. They had all been fasting, but what was Paul's advice for them to do?

5. How many were on ship and how did they get to safety?

6. How is Leviticus 16:29 in the Old Testament like Acts of the Apostles 27:9 in the New Testament?

7. Write a note to the Holy Spirit and ask for the wisdom to make good choices.

The Word of God is BEYOND AWESOME!

Verse of the Chapter: Acts of the Apostles 28:28
"Let it be known to you that this salvation of God has been sent to the Gentiles; they will listen."

QUESTIONS AND RESPONSES

1. Where did Paul and his companions finally reach?

2. What did Paul do for the sick people on this island?

3. After winter they set sail again. Where was it that they arrived and Paul thanked God and took courage?

4. What did Paul say in his testimony to the Jews in Rome?

5. What did Paul do in the two full years he stayed in Rome?

6. How is Isaiah 6:10 in the Old Testament like Acts of the Apostles 28:27 in the New Testament?

7. Write a note to God, the Father, about your needs and your wants...

FOCUS ON THE "WORD" WITH RESPONSES OR ANSWERS

Matthew 1

QUESTIONS AND RESPONSES

1. How many generations are there from Abraham to the Messiah?

   14 x 3 = 42 generations Verse 1:17

2. What does the word, "genealogy" mean?

   Genealogy is the continuity of God's providential plan, the ancestors. Verses 1-2:23 (notes)

3. Who is the Messiah?

   Jesus is the Messiah. Verse 1:17 (notes)

4. What does betrothed mean?

   Betrothal was the first part of the marriage like an engagement of today. Verse 1:18 (notes)

5. What dream is in the Old Testament: Genesis 37:5-11?

   In the Old Testament we have the dream of Joseph communicating with God similar to the dream of Joseph in the New Testament, Matthew 1:20. Verse 1:20 (notes)

Matthew 2

QUESTIONS AND RESPONSES

1. Who are the Magi?

   Magi are astrologers who were known as having more than human knowledge. Verse 2:1 (notes)

2. Where did Joseph and Mary go in order to be safe from King Herod?

   Joseph and Mary went to Egypt. Verse 2:13

3. What did King Herod do that was evil?

   He ordered the massacre of all the boys in Bethlehem and its vicinity that were the age of two and under. Verse 2:16

4. How is the Old Testament, Numbers 24:17, like Matthew 2:2 in the New Testament?

   The reference of "the star" meant that the ruler, the King, was born.

5. In the New Testament, Matthew 2:20 is parallel with the verse in the Old Testament, Exodus 4:19. What is this verse about?

   Both verses state: "for all the men who sought your life are dead".

Matthew 3

QUESTIONS AND RESPONSES

1. What does it mean to repent?

    Repent is to have a change of heart and conduct. It is a turning of one's life from rebellion to obedience toward God. Verse 3:2 (notes)

2. What does it mean to produce good fruit?

    To produce good fruit means to repent and to do good. Verse 3:8

3. In what river were a lot of people including Jesus baptized?

    A lot of people were baptized in the Jordan River as well as Jesus. Verse 3:13

4. Who was John the Baptist?

    John the Baptist was the one who baptized Jesus when he came from Galilee to fulfill all righteousness. This means to submit to the plan of God. Verses 3:14-15 and (notes)

5. What is written in the Old Testament, Psalm 2:7, that relates to this chapter?

    It is similar to verse 3:17 in Matthew that says: "This is my beloved Son, with whom I am well pleased."

Matthew 4

QUESTIONS AND RESPONSES

1. How long did Jesus fast in the desert?

    Jesus fasted forty days and forty nights in the desert. Verse 4:2

2. Who tested Jesus in the desert?

    The devil tested Jesus. Verses 4:5-7.

3. Who are the four apostles called in Matthew 4:18-22?

    The names of the four apostles that are called in these verses are: Peter, Andrew, James and John.

4. What did Jesus do in Galilee?

    In Galilee Jesus taught in the synagogues, proclaimed the Gospel and cured every disease and illness. Verse 4:23

5. How is the verse from the Old Testament: Exodus 24:18 similar to Matthew 4:2?

    They both have forty days and forty nights in. In the New Testament Jesus fasted that long. In the Old Testament Moses went up to the mountain that long.

Matthew 5

QUESTIONS AND RESPONSES

1. The Sermon on the Mount is called, what?

    The Sermon on the Mount is called: "The Beatitudes". Verse 5:2

2. Whoever breaks one of the least of the commandments and teaches others to do so, they will be called what?

    They will be called least in the kingdom of heaven. Verse 5:19

3. What advice have we been given about taking an oath?

    We are not to take a false oath. Verse 5:33

4. What advice have we been given about loving our enemies?

    We are to love our enemies and pray for those who persecute us. Verse 5:44

5. How is Exodus 20:13 (Old Testament) like Matthew 5:21 (New Testament)?

    They both state that: "You shall not kill."

Matthew 6

QUESTIONS AND RESPONSES

1. What is almsgiving?

   Almsgiving is giving donations or doing good deeds. Verses 6:1-4

2. What prayer is in this chapter that we say at Mass?

   The Our Father is said at Mass. Verse 6:9

3. What does it mean: "Where your treasure is, there also your heart is".

   This statement implies the question: Rather your treasure is in getting wealthy or getting to heaven? Verses 6:19-20

4. What are we to seek first each and every day of our lives?

   We are to seek first the kingdom of God and His righteousness. Verse 6:33

5. How is Matthew 6:16 in the New Testament like Leviticus 16:29 in the Old Testament? Both verses are about fasting. The Old Testament is about fasting from work and the New Testament is about fasting from food.

Matthew 7

QUESTIONS AND RESPONSES

1. Are we to ask God for things?

   Yes, we are to ask God for things. verse 7:7

2. What is the Golden Rule?

   The Golden Rule is: "Do to others whatever you would have them do to you." Verse 7:12

3. What gate are we to choose the narrow or the wide? Why?

   We are to choose the narrow gate because it is constricted and leads to life. Verse 7:14

4. Who will be like a wise man who built his house on rock?

   The person who will be like a wise man is the one who listens to the Word of God and acts on it. verse 7:24

5. Why is the Psalm 6:9 in the Old Testament like Matthew 7:23 in the New Testament?

   These verses are alike because they both mention evildoers.

Matthew 8

QUESTIONS AND RESPONSES

1. Who had faith in this chapter of Matthew?

    The centurion had faith. Verse 8:10

2. What does it mean when it says that Peter's mother-in-law was cured?

    Peter's mother-in-law was sick with a fever, but after Jesus touched her, the fever left her. verses 8:14-15

3. When were the apostles terrified? What did Jesus do?

    The apostles were terrified when they were in a boat during a violent storm. Jesus asked them why they were terrified, then got up and rebuked the winds and the sea. verse 8:26

4. Who preached and worked miracles in Galilee?

    Jesus preached and worked miracles in Galilee. Verses 8:3, 8:13, 8:15, 8:17, 8:22, 8:26, 8:32

5. How is Matthew 8:1-4 in the New Testament like Leviticus 14:2-9 in the Old Testament?

    Both readings are about the cure of a leper.

Matthew 9

QUESTIONS AND RESPONSES

1.   What disciple did Jesus tell: "Follow me"?

     Jesus called Matthew. verse 9:9

2.   What kind of people did Jesus eat with?

     Jesus ate with sinners. verse 9:11

3.   Name two healings that Jesus performed?

     Jesus performed the healing of two blind men and the healing of a mute person. Verses 9:29 and 9:33

4.   What healing do you like the best?

     PERSONAL THOUGHTS AND/OR FEELINGS

5.   Daniel 12:2 in the Old Testament is like Matthew 9:24 in the New Testament, in what way?

     They both mention someone who is sleeping

Matthew 10

QUESTIONS AND RESPONSES

1. Name the twelve apostles.

    Peter, Andrew, James, John, Philip, Bartholomew, Thomas, Matthew, James, Thaddeus, Simon and Judas Verses 10:2-4

2. What is the proclamation that Jesus asks the apostles to give?

    The proclamation that Jesus asks the apostles to give is: "The kingdom of heaven is at hand. Cure the sick, raise the dead, cleanse lepers, drive out demons. Without cost you have received; without cost you give." Verses 10:7-8

3. What are we to do if someone insults us for believing in Jesus?

    If someone insults us or persecutes us for believing in Jesus, flee to another town. Verse 10:23

4. Who is being mentioned in Matthew 10:41?

    A prophet and a righteous man are mentioned in this verse.

5. How is Exodus 4:12 in the Old Testament like Matthew 1:20 in the New Testament?

    Both verses are about speaking,

Matthew 11

QUESTIONS AND RESPONSES

1. Who is John the Baptist?

    John the Baptist was a prophet. verse 11:9-10 (notes)

2. Who ate with tax collectors and sinners?

    The Son of Man ate with tax collectors and sinners. verse 11:19

3. What did Jesus give to the Father?

    Jesus gave praise to the Father. verse 11:25

4. What are we to take to Jesus in prayer?

    We are to take our burdens in prayer to Jesus. verse 11:28

5. What is being said in the Old Testament, Jeremiah 6:16 and in the

    New Testament Matthew 11:29? If we go the way of good, we will find
    rest for our souls.

Matthew 12

QUESTIONS AND RESPONSES

1. What did Jesus do on the Sabbath?

    On the Sabbath, Jesus and his disciples went through a field of grain, Verse 12:1

2. Why did Jesus do this on the Sabbath?

    Jesus did this on the Sabbath because the disciples were without food and that made the violation of the law permissible. Verses 12:5-6 and (notes)

3. What does a good person bring forth?

    A good person brings forth good out of a store of goodness. Verse 12:35

4. What will happen on the day of judgment?

    At the final judgment the faithless generation will be condemned for rejecting Jesus. Verses 12:41-42 (notes)

5. What does Exodus 34:21 in the Old Testament say that is like Mattbew 12:1-2 in the New Testament?

    The seventh day or the Sabbath day is to be a day of rest.

Matthew 13

QUESTIONS AND RESPONSES

1. Name three parables.

   The Parable of the Sower, The Parable of the Weeds among the Wheat, The Parable of the Mustard Seed verses: 13:1-9 and 13:24-30 and 13:31-32

2. What is the purpose of parables?

   The purpose of parables is so that the crowd will understand. Verse 13:13

3. What is the message in the parable of the sower?

   In the parable of the sower, the message is that the seed sown on rich soil is the one who hears the word and understands it, who indeed bears fruit. Verse 13:23

4. What is the message in the parable of the mustard seed?

   The message in the parable of the mustard seed is the amazing contrast between the small beginnings of the kingdom and its marvelous expansion. Verses 13:31-33 (notes)

5. How is Matthew 13:35 in the New Testament like Psalm 78:2 in the Old Testament?

   Both verses state: "I will open my mouth in a parable or parables."

Matthew 14

QUESTIONS AND RESPONSES

1. Who was responsible for the death of John the Baptist?

    Herod and the daughter of Herodias are responsible for the death of John the Baptist. Verses 14:6-

2. Name two miracles in this chapter.

    Two miracles in this chapter are: The Feeding of the Five Thousand and The Walking on the Water. Verses 14:13-21 and 14:22-33

3. What did the people of Gennesaret beg?

    The people of Gennesaret begged to touch the tassel on the cloak of Jesus so that they might be healed. Verse 14:36

4. What is the fourth watch of the night?

    The fourth watch of the night for the Romans is between 3 am and 6 am. Verse 14:25 (notes)

5. How is 2 Kings 4:42-44 in the Old Testament like Matthew 14:13-21 in the New Testament?

    Both passages talk about the multiplication of loaves.

Matthew 15

QUESTIONS AND RESPONSES

1. What commandment is stated in this chapter?

   "Honor your father and your mother", the fourth commandment, is in this chapter. Verse 15:4

2. What woman had great faith?

   The Canaanite woman had great faith. verse 15:28

3. Three healings of Jesus are:

   Healing the mute, healing the blind and healing the lame. verse 15:31

4. Why did Jesus want to feed the crowds?

   Jesus wanted to feed the crowds because they had been with Him for three days and had nothing to eat. Verse 15:32

5. What message is in Exodus 20:12 in the Old Testament is like Matthew 15:4 in the New Testament?

   Both verses state: "Honor your father and your mother."

Matthew 16

QUESTIONS AND RESPONSES

1. Who were the Pharisees and Sadducces?

    They were teachers who tested Jesus and corrupted others in their teach-ings. They were evil and expected a sign from Jesus. Verses 16:1 and 4 and the note from verse 12

2. Who did Jesus give the keys to the kingdom of heaven to?

    Jesus gave the keys to the kingdom of heaven to Peter. Verse 16:19

3. Who said this: "Whoever wishes to come after me must deny himself, take up his cross, and follow me."

    These words were said by Jesus. Verse 16:24

4. Who was this said to: "Whoever wishes to come after me must deny him-self, take up his cross, and follow me."

    These words were said to Jesus' disciples. Verse 16:24

5. Who is mentioned in Matthew verse 16:14 in the New Testament and also the Old Testament, Malachi 3:23?

    Elijah is mentioned in both of the above verses.

Matthew 17

QUESTIONS AND RESPONSES

1. Describe the Transfiguration of Jesus.

    Jesus' face shined like the sun and His clothes were as white as light. Verse 17:2

2. What is important for healing to take place?

    It is important to have faith for healing to take place. Verse 17:20

3. Where did the disciples gather?

    The disciples gathered in Galilee. verse 17:22

4. What did Jesus compare faith to?

    Jesus compared faith to a mustard seed. verse 17:20

5. What does Matthew 17:1 in the New Testament mention that is like Exodus 24:12 in the Old Testament?

    They both speak of the mountain.

Matthew 18

QUESTIONS AND RESPONSES

1. Who is the greatest in the kingdom of heaven?

    A child is the greatest in the kingdom of heaven. verse 18:2

2. Name two parables in this chapter.

    Two parables in this chapter are: The Parable of the Lost Sheep and The Parable of the Unforgiving Servant. Titles of verses 18:10 and 21.

3. What are you to do if your brother sins?

    If your brother sins, go and tell him. If he doesn't listen, take two or three along and tell him. If he refuses, tell the church. Verses 18:15-17

4. If two or three are praying together, who is in their midst?

    If two or three are praying together, Jesus is in their midst. Verse 18:20

5. How is Matthew 18:22 in the New Testament like Genesis 4:24 in the Old Testament?

    They both mention Seven or Seventy-seven.

Matthew 19

QUESTIONS AND RESPONSES

1. What did Jesus do for the children?

   Jesus placed His hands on the children and blessed them. verse 19:1

2. What answer did Jesus give when he was asked: "What good must I do to gain eternal life?"

   Jesus said: "Why do you ask me about the good? There is only One who is good. If you wish to enter into life, keep the commandments." verse 19:17

3. (Complete the sentence.) It is easier for a camel to pass through an eye...

   of a needle, than for one who is rich to enter the kingdom of God. Verse 19:24

4. What will those who have given up house, family and land to follow Jesus receive?

   These people will receive a hundred times more and will inherit eternal life. Verse 19:29

5. What is in the Old Testament Exodus 20:12-16 that is like Matthew 19:18-19 in the New Testament?

   These are the Ten Commandments.

Matthew 20

QUESTIONS AND RESPONSES

1. Why did Jesus say: "Are you envious because I am generous?"

    Jesus said these words because He noticed resentment, when He was generous to others. Verse 20:15

2. What prediction was Jesus giving?

    Jesus was predicting His death. verse 20:1

3. What did Jesus mean when He said: "He did not come to be served but to serve and to give His life as a ransom for many?"

    Jesus came to save us from our sins. Verse 20:28

4. What did Jesus do for the two blind men?

    Jesus touched the eyes of the blind men and they immediately received their sight. Verse 20:34

5. How is the verse in the Old Testament of 1 Kings 1:11 like Matthew 20:20 in the New Testament? The mother of the sons are words in both verses.

Matthew 21

QUESTIONS AND RESPONSES

1. Whose entry was made into Jerusalem? Describe it.

   Jesus entry was made into Jerusalem, People laid their cloaks on the road and some cut branches and laid them on the road. Verse 21:8

2. What was taking place in the Temple?

   Selling and buying was the action in the Temple. verse 21:12

3. What message did you get from the Parable of the Two Sons?

   The message from the Parable of the Two Sons is about faith and not judging others. verse 21:32

4. What message did you get from the Parable of the Tenants?

   The message from the Parable of the Tenants is to treat all people right and to produce good fruit. verse 21:43

5. How is the verse in the Old Testament of Psalm 8:3 like Matthew 21:16 in the New Testament?

   Out of the mouths of infants and nurslings you have brought forth praise.

Matthew 22

QUESTIONS AND RESPONSES

1. What is a message from the Parable of the wedding Feast?

    The message is that many are invited and few are chosen. Verse 22:14

2. Who are the hypocrites in this chapter?

    The hypocrites are the Pharisees, their disciples and the Herodians that they had asked to go with them to test Jesus. Verses 22:15-16

3. At the resurrection of the body from the dead, it will be like, what?

    At the resurrection all will be like the angels in heaven. Verse 22:30

4. What is the greatest commandment?

    The greatest commandment is: "You shall love the Lord your God, with all your heart, with all your soul and with all your mind." Verse 22:37

5. What similarities are there in the verse from the Old Testament of Daniel 12:2 with Matthew 22:23 in the New Testament?

    These verses mention the resurrection.

Matthew 23

QUESTIONS AND RESPONSES

1. Who are the hypocrites in this chapter?

    The hypocrites in this chapter are the scribes and Pharisees. Verse 23:2

2. Name two things the hypocrites did?

    The two things that hypocrites did were: They preached, but did not practice what they preached. They put heavy burdens on others, but did not lift a finger to help. Verses 23:3-4

3. What are the blind to do?

    The blind are to believe in heaven and the throne of God. Verse 23:22

4. What people were murdered?

    The people that were murdered were: the prophets, Abel and Zachariah. Verse 23:31 and 35

5. How does Deuteronomy 14:22 in the Old Testament compare with Matthew 23:23 in the New Testament?

    These verses state that people are to pay tithes.

Matthew 24

QUESTIONS AND RESPONSES

1. What Mount was Jesus at in this chapter and who was there with Him?

    Jesus was at the Mount of Olives and the disciples were with Him. Verse 24:3

2. What is the coming of the Son of Man to be like?

    The coming of the Son of Man is to be like the sun being darkened, the moon with no light, stars falling from the sky and the powers of heaven shaken, Verse 24:29

3. What is the lesson of the fig tree?

    The words of Jesus will not pass away. verse 24:35

4. What kind of hour will it be when the Son of Man comes?

    The hour when the Son of Man comes will not be known. verse 24:36

5. How is Matthew 24:30 in the New Testament like Zechariah 12:12 in the Old Testament?

    The main word in the verses is mourn.

Matthew 25

QUESTIONS AND RESPONSES

1. What is the message in the parable of the ten virgins?

    The message in the parable of the ten virgins is: to stay awake because we do not know when the lord is coming again. Verse 25:13

2. What is the message in the parable of the talents?

    The message in the parable of the talents is: the wicked and lazy will be thrown outside in the darkness (hell). verse 25:30

3. What is the message in the story of the Judgment of the Nations?

    The message in the story of the Judgment of the nation is: the righteous will get eternal life. verse 25:46b

4. Name two or more things that we should do to gain eternal life stated in this chapter?

    Things that we need to do to gain eternal life are: give food to the hungry, take care of the ill and welcome a stranger. Verses 25:37-3

5. How is Matthew 25:31 in the New Testament like Daniel 7:13 in the Old Testament?

    Both verses are about the son of man coming.

Matthew 26

QUESTIONS AND RESPONSES

1. Who betrayed Jesus and how much was he willing to turn Jesus over for?

   Judas betrayed Jesus and was willing to turn Him over thirty pieces of silver. Verses 26:14 and 15

2. What happened at the Lord's Supper?

   At the Last Supper Jesus took the bread and said the blessing. Then He took the cup, gave thanks and gave it to the disciples. Verses 26:26 and 27

3. Who said: "Even though I should have to die with you, I will not deny you." and what happened?

   Peter said that he would not deny Jesus, but he did deny Him three times. Verses 26:69-74

4. What did Jesus do in Gethsemane?

   Jesus prayed in Gethsemane. Verse 26:36

5. How is Zechariah 13:7 in the Old Testament similar to Matthew 26:31 in the New Testament?

   They have the same words: strike the shepherd and the sheep will be dispersed.

Matthew 27

QUESTIONS AND RESPONSES

1. How did Judas die?

   Judas went off and hung himself. verse 27:5

2. Who was released instead of Jesus?

   Barabbas was released instead of Jesus. verse 27:26

3. Who mocked and crucified Jesus?

   The soldiers mocked and crucified Jesus. verses 27:27-31

4. Who were some of the women present at the death of Jesus?

   Some of the women who were present at the death of Jesus were: Mary Magdalene, Mary (the mother of James and Joseph) and the mother of the sons of Zebedee. Verse 27:56

5. How is Matthew 27:47 in the New Testament like the reading in 2 Kings 2:11 in the Old Testament?

   These verses mention Elijah being taken up to heaven.

Matthew 28

QUESTIONS and RESPONSE

1. Who came to the tomb on the first day after the Sabbath?

    Mary Magdalene and the other Mary came to the tomb on the first day
    after the Sabbath. verse 28:1

2. What did the angel say when they came to the tomb?

    When they came to the tomb, the angel said: "Do not be afraid." verse
    28:10a

3. Where did the eleven disciples go?

    The eleven disciples went to Galilee to the mountain. verse 28:16

4. What did Jesus tell the disciples to go and do?

    Jesus told the disciples to go to all nations make disciples and baptize.
    verse 28:19

5. How is the verse of Daniel 7:14 in the Old Testament like Matthew 28:20
    in the New Testament?

    These verses state that kingship will be always.

Mark 1

QUESTIONS FOR REFLECTION AND RESPONSE

1. What was an important sacrament in the beginning of Jesus' Ministry? Why?

    Baptism was an important sacrament of the beginning of Jesus' ministry. Jesus identifies Himself with the people by being baptized. This is divine intervention. Verse 1:8

2. What might we need to leave in order to follow Jesus more faithfully?

    In order to follow Jesus more faithfully, we might need to leave work and family. Verses 1:18 and 20

3. What are two cures by Jesus and what meaning do they have for me?

    Jesus cured the demoniac and Simon's mother-in-law. Verses 1:25 and 31
    PERSONAL THOUGHTS AND/OR FEELINGS

4. Where did Jesus often go and for what reason? Do I do this?

    Jesus often went to pray in a deserted area or a mountain. Verse 1:35
    PERSONAL THOUGHTS AND/OR FEELNGS

5. How is the passage in Numbers 12:10 of the Old Testament like Mark 1:40 of the New Testament?

    They are about a leper.

Mark 2

QUESTIONS FOR REFLECTION AND RESPONSE

1. How did the people feel about the healing of the paralytic?

    The people were astounded and glorified God saying: "We have never seen anything like this." Verse 2:12

2. Who did Jesus eat dinner with?

    Jesus ate dinner with tax collectors and sinners. Verse 2:16

3. How do I handle the question of fasting?

    PERSONAL THOUGHTS AND/OR FEELINGS

4. How do I handle the question of what is unlawful on the Sabbath?

    PERSONAL THOUGHTS AND/OR FEELINGS

5. How is Leviticus 24:9 in the Old Testament like Mark 2:25-26 in the New Testament?

    Both verses are about the eating of the bread.

Mark 3

QUESTIONS FOR REFLECTION AND RESPONSE

1. Why did Jesus cure the man with a withered hand on the Sabbath?

   Jesus cured the man with the withered hand on the Sabbath because it is better to do good than evil. It is better to save life rather than destroy it. Verse 3:4

2. What is interesting about the Mission of the Twelve?

   Jesus called the Twelve after going to the mountain. This is associated with solemn moments. Verse 3:13

3. How did Jesus speak to the crowds?

   Jesus spoke to the crowds in parables. verse 3:23

4. Who does Jesus say His family is?

   Jesus said that his family is those who do the will of the Father, Verse 3:35

5. How is Matthew 10:1-4 in the New Testament like Mark 3:13-18 in the New Testament?

   The Mission of the Twelve is the theme for both verses.

Mark 4

QUESTIONS FOR REFLECTION AND RESPONSE

1. What message do I personally hear from the parable of the sower?

   PERSONAL THOUGHTS AND/OR FEELINGS

2. What message do I personally hear from the parable of the lamp?

   PERSONAL THOUGHTS AND/OR FEELINGS

3. What message do I personally hear from the parable of the mustard seed?

   PERSONAL THOUGHTS AND/OR FEELINGS

4. What message do I personally hear from the passage of the Calming of the Storm?

   PERSONAL THOUGHTS AND/OR FEELINGS

5. How is the passage from the Old Testament of Ezekiel 17:23 like the passage from Mark 4:32 in the New Testament?

   They both speak of the branches that grow and the birds that enjoy them.

Mark 5

QUESTIONS FOR REFLECTION AND RESPONSE

1. What happened to the possessed man? How would I have reacted?

    The demons came out of him and they went into the herd of the swine. Verse 5:13 PERSONAL THOUGHTS AND/OR FEELINGS

2. What saved the woman in this chapter?

    Jesus saved the woman in this chapter because she touched His cloak and had faith. Verse 5:34

3. What cure did I like the best in this chapter? Why?

    PERSONAL THOUGHTS AND/OR FEELINGS

4. How is Mark 5:39 of the New Testament like Matthew 27:52 of the New Testament?

    The verses were about a body that was raised to life.

5. How is Mark 5:39 of the New Testament like John 11:11 of the New Testament?

    The verses were about a person being asleep and then waking up to life.

Mark 6

QUESTIONS FOR REFLECTION AND RESPONSE

1. What did the people of Nazareth lack when Jesus was teaching in the synagogues? Why?

   When Jesus was teaching in the synagogues the people lacked faith. They had asked if He was the carpenter's son and if his brothers and sisters were there with them, too. Verses 6:3 and 6

2. What did Jesus give the apostles?

   Jesus gave the apostles authority over unclean spirits. Verse 6:7

3. What insight did I get from the death of John the Baptist?

   PERSONAL THOUGHTS AND/OR FEELINGS

4. What was fascinating when Jesus and the apostles were working together?

   PERSONAL THOUGHTS AND/OR FEELINGS

5. How is Isaiah 43:1 of the Old Testament like Mark 6:50 of the New Testament?

   Both verses are saying not to be afraid.

Mark 7

QUESTIONS FOR REFLECTION AND RESPONSE

1. What was a tradition of the Elders?

   A tradition of the Elders was to wash hands before eating. verse 7:3

2. What did Jesus teach that is important?

   Jesus taught that we are to keep the commandments. verse 7:8

3. What was significant about the Syrophoenician woman's faith?

   This woman was Greek and begged Jesus to drive out the demon in her daughter. She was persistent in her belief of Jesus. verses 7:26 and 28

4. What was significant about the healing of the deaf man?

   The significant thing about the healing of the deaf man was that Jesus took him away from the crowd of people and healed him. verses 7:33-35

5. How is Matthew 11:5-6 in the New Testament like Mark 7:36 in the New Testament?

   Both verses are about the proclaiming of Jesus' miracles.

Mark 8

QUESTIONS FOR REFLECTION AND RESPONSE

1. What are the similarities of Mark 6:34-44 and Mark 8:1-10 in the New Testament?

   In chapter 6 of Mark, the reading is about feeding the five thousand with twelve baskets leftover. In chapter 8 of Mark, the reading is about the feeding of the four thousand with seven baskets leftover.

2. Do I ever expect a sign from Heaven like the Pharisees did?

   PERSONAL THOUGHTS AND/OR FEELINGS

3. What happened at Bethsaida and what significance does this have in my life?

   In Bethsaida a blind man was healed. verse 8:25 PERSONAL THOUGHTS AND/OR FEELINGS

4. What are some conditions for discipleship?

   Some of the conditions for discipleship are to deny oneself, take up one's cross and follow Jesus. verse 8:34

5. How is Numbers 14:11 in the Old Testament like Mark 8:11 in the New Testament?

   People were expecting signs.

Mark 9

QUESTIONS FOR REFLECTION AND RESPONSE

1. What message is in the passage on the Transfiguration of Jesus?

   We need to listen to Jesus who is always with us. verse 9:7

2. Why couldn't the disciples drive the demon out of the boy?

   The disciples couldn't drive the demon out of the boy because they did not pray enough. verse 9:29

3. Who does Jesus say will be the greatest in the kingdom of heaven?

   Jesus said that anyone who receives a child in the name of Jesus receives me; and whoever receives me, receives not me but the One who sent me. Verse 9:37

4. What is to happen, if we cause one of these little ones to sin?

   If we cause one of these little ones to sin, we will go to hell. verses 9:42-43

5. How is Mark 9:9-13 of the New Testament like Malachi 3:23-24 of the Old Testament?

   They both talk about Elijah, the prophet.

Mark 10

QUESTIONS FOR REFLECTION AND RESPONSE

1. How do we need to accept the kingdom of God?

    We accept the kingdom of God like a child. verse 10:14

2. What must we do to inherit eternal life?

    To inherit eternal life we must have total dependence upon the gospel and total obedience to it. The note of Verse 10:15

3. What did the Third Prediction include?

    The Third Prediction included the following: Jesus being condemned, handed over to the Gentiles, put to death and rose on the third day. verses 10:33 and 34

4. Why did the Son of Man come?

    The Son of Man came to serve and give His life. verse 10:45

5. What in the New Testament, Mark 10:23, is similar to Isaiah 3:10 of the Old Testament?

    In the Old Testament material goods were a sign of God's favor and in New Testament wealth makes it hard to enter heaven. Both verses are about material goods.

Mark 11

QUESTIONS FOR REFLECTION AND RESPONSE

1. What was the entry into Jerusalem like?

   The Entry into Jerusalem was a welcome of Jesus, the prophet. Verses 11:8-10

2. What is the Temple to be called?

   The Temple is to be called a house of prayer. verse 11:17

3. What is a message Jesus gives Peter in regard to the withered fig tree?

   The message that Jesus gives Peter in regards to the fig tree is: to have faith, pray, and forgive others. verses 11:22-25

4. Who questioned the authority of Jesus?

   The chief priests, the scribes and the elders questioned the authority of Jesus. Verse 11:27

5. How is the verse in the Old Testament of Hosea 2:14 like the verse in the New Testament of Mark 11:13?

   They are both about fig trees.

Mark 12

QUESTIONS FOR REFLECTION AND RESPONSE

1. What is the message in the parable of the tenants?

    A message in this parable of the tenants is to have respect and to read the scriptures. Verses 12:6 and 10

2. What is a message in the passage of paying taxes to the emperor?

    A message in paying taxes is to be truthful to everyone. Verses 12:14 and 17

3. What is the Greatest Commandment?

    The Greatest Commandment is to love God with all our heart, mind, soul and strength and to love others as ourselves. verses 12:30 and 31

4. What is a message in the passage of the poor widow's contribution?

    The message in this passage is that we are to make sacrifices when we give contributions to others. verse 12:44

5. How is Psalm 110:1 in the Old Testament like Mark 12:36 in the New Testament?

    Psalm: The Lord says to my lord: "Take your throne at my right hand, while I make your enemies my footstool. Mark: The Lord said to my lord, "Sit at my right hand until I place your enemies under your feet."

Mark 13

QUESTIONS FOR REFLECTION AND RESPONSE

1. What are signs of the end??

   Some of the signs of the end times are: wars, earthquakes and famine. verses 13:7 and 8

2. How will the Son of Man come?

   The Son of Man will be in the clouds, when the sun darkens, the moon has no light and the stars are falling. verses 13:24 - 26

3. What is the lesson of the fig tree?

   The lesson of the fig tree is to know that the Son of Man is near. Verse 13:29

4. Why do we need to be watchful?

   We need to be watchful because no one knows the day or the hour the Lord is coming. verse 13:35

5. How is the passage in the New Testament of Mark 13:26 like the passage in the Old Testament in Exodus 34:5?

   The verses both contain the line on the Lord coming down in the cloud.

Mark 14

QUESTIONS FOR REFLECTION AND RESPONSE

1. What was significant about the woman at Bethany?

    The woman at Bethany loved Jesus very much. verses 14:8 and 9

2. Who was the betrayer and what did he do?

    The betrayer of Jesus is Judas. Judas handed Jesus over to the chief priests to be arrested. verses 14:43-45

3. What was significant about the Lord's Supper?

    At the Lord's Supper, Jesus sacrificed His Body and Blood. Verses 14:22-24

4. What insight did I get from the passage of the Agony in the Garden?

    PERSONAL THOUGHTS AND/OR FEELINGS

5. How is the passage from the Old Testament of Deuteronomy 16:1-8 like the passage in the New Testament of Mark 14:1?

    Both passages are about the Passover and Feast of the Unleavened Bread.

Mark 15

QUESTIONS FOR REFLECTION AND RESPONSE

1. What was significant for me in the sentence of the death of Jesus?

    PERSONAL THOUGHTS AND/OR FEELINGS

2. What was significant for me in the passage of the crucifixion?

    PERSONAL THOUGHTS AND/OR FEELINGS

3. What was significant for me in the passage on the actual death of Jesus?

    PERSONAL THOUGHTS AND/OR FEELINGS

4. What was significant for me in the passage on the actual burial of Jesus?

    PERSONAL THOUGHTS AND/OR FEELINGS

5. How is the verse from the Old Testament of Psalm 22:2 like the verse from the New Testament of Mark 15:34?

    Old Testament: "My God, my God, why have you forsaken me?" New Testament: "My God, my God, why have you abandoned me?"

Mark 16

QUESTIONS FOR REFLECTION AND RESPONSE

1. What insight or verse tells me that Jesus rose from the dead?

    In verse 16:6 it says that Jesus has been raised,

2. "If you do not believe, you have a hardness of heart." What could this mean? verse 16:14 (If you do not believe, you will not be saved).

    PERSONAL THOUGHTS AND/OR FEELINGS

3. Matthew 28:1-10, Mark 16:1-8 and Luke 24:1-12 are all about what?

    How are they alike? These verses are about the Resurrection of Jesus.

4. What are some differences from the passages from question 3?

    Matthew's Gospel states: "Do not be afraid". Mark's Gospel states: "They were afraid". Luke's Gospel states: "Peter went home amazed".

5. What was significant to me about the Ascension of Jesus?

    Jesus was taken to heaven and was seated at the right hand of the Father. The disciples then went and preached everywhere. Verses 16:19 and 20

Luke 1

QUESTIONS AND RESPONSES

1. What seemed of importance in the passage of the Announcement of the Birth of John?

   The angels were saying not to be afraid. The prayers of Zechariah and Elizabeth were answered. They would have joy and gladness. Verses 1:13 and 14

2. What seemed of importance in the passage of the Announcement of the Birth of Jesus? .

   Jesus would be the Son of God because nothing is impossible with God. Verses 1:35-37

3. What is the name of the passage read every evening by clergy, religious and lay people as the prayer of the Church, Luke 1:46-56?

   This prayer of the Church is called the Canticle of Mary

4. What is the name of the passage read every morning by clergy, religious and lay people as the prayer of the Church, Luke 1:67-80?

   This prayer of the Church is called the Canticle of Zechariah.

5. What is the meaning in the verse of Luke 1:69 of the New Testament and is like the verse of Psalm 18:3 in the Old Testament?

   They both talk about a horn for our salvation.

Luke 2

QUESTIONS AND RESPONSES

1. What seemed of importance in the passage on the Birth of Jesus?

    Jesus, our Savior, is the great joy and good news verse 2:10

2. What was the most significant part of the visit of the Shepherds?

    The shepherds were believers because they glorified and praised God. verse 2:20

3. Why was there a Presentation of Jesus in the Temple?

    In those days there was the Law of Moses in which every first born son was consecrated and to offer the sacrifice of two turtledoves or pigeons at the Temple. Verses 2:22-24

4. What did Jesus do in the Temple when He was a boy? Why?

    When Jesus was a boy, He went with His family to the Passover each year. He listened to teachers and asked them questions and others were amazed at His understanding. Verse 2:46

5. What is similar between the passage in the Old Testament in Wisdom 7:4-6 and the passage in the New Testament of Luke 2:7?

    Both passages say: He was wrapped in swaddling clothes.

Luke 3

QUESTIONS AND RESPONSES

1. What seemed of importance in the passage on the preaching of John the Baptist?

    It seems like it is important for people to change their lives and live to do good. Verse 3:8

2. What happened at the Baptism of Jesus?

    At the Baptism of Jesus heaven was opened up when all were praying and the Holy Spirit came upon Him. A voice from heaven said: "You are my beloved Son; with You I am well pleased." Verses 3:21 and 22

3. Why was Jesus baptized?

    Jesus was baptized because it was a part of His preparation for ministry and for the preaching and teaching for all who want salvation. Verse 3:21, note

4. What are my thoughts on the Genealogy of Jesus?

    PERSONAL THOUGHTS AND/OR FEELINGS

5. How is the verse Psalm 2:7 of the Old Testament like Luke 3:22 of the New Testament?

    Both verses state: "You are my Son."

Luke 4

QUESTIONS AND ANSWERS

1. What seemed of importance in the passage on the Temptation of Jesus?

    Jesus was persistent in not giving into the temptations of the devil. Verse 4:13

2. Where did Jesus go to begin His Ministry?

    Jesus went to Galilee and Nazareth to begin His ministry. Verses 4:14 and 16

3. What happened at Nazareth when Jesus preached?

    Jesus read a scroll from the prophet Isaiah and all were amazed. Then they drove Him out of town. verses 4:17 and 29

4. What were some of the healings or cures in this chapter?

    Some of the healings and cures in this chapter are: the cure of the demoniac and the cure of Simon's mother-in-law. Titles of verses 4:31 and 38

5. How is the verse Deuteronomy 8:2 of the Old Testament like Luke 4:2 of the New Testament? Forty years is in the Old Testament and forty days is in the New Testament.

Luke 5

QUESTIONS AND RESPONSES

1. What was significant in the passage of the call of Simon Peter, the fisher-
    man?

    It is quite significant that Simon Peter makes the choice to leave every-
    thing and follow Jesus. Verse 5:11

2. What was the story about when Jesus called Matthew, Levi, the tax col-
    lector?

    It was about Jesus calling sinners not the righteous. Verse 5:32

3. What are two cures or healings in this chapter?

    Two healings in this chapter are: the cure of the leper and the healing of
    the paralytic. Verses 5:13 and 24

4. What was Jesus' teaching concerning fasting in this chapter?

    Jesus was telling the people that while He is with them, they did not need
    to fast. Verse 5:34

5. How is the verse in the New Testament Luke 5:14 like the verse in Le-
    viticus 14:2 of the Old Testament?

    These verses are about being brought to the priest for cleansing or puri-
    fication.

Luke 6

QUESTIONS AND RESPONSES

1. The Sabbath is a day for rest, but what are two deeds that are more important?

   Two deeds that are better than resting on the Sabbath are feeding the hungry and healing the sick. It is better to do good rather than evil and it is better to save life rather than destroy. Verse 6:9

2. How many disciples did Jesus call? Who became a traitor?

   Jesus called twelve disciples and Judas was the traitor. Verses 6:13 and 16

3. Why did people want to touch Jesus?

   People wanted to touch Jesus to receive His power and to be healed. Verse 6:19

4. What are the differences and similarities of Luke 6:20-26 and Matthew 5:1-12?

   In Luke we have the Sermon on the Plain and in Matthew we have the Sermon on the Mount.

5. What does Jesus say about the one who listens and acts and the one who listens and does not act?

   The one who listens and acts has a foundation, The one who does not listen and act does not have a foundation. Verses 6:48 and 49

Luke 7

QUESTIONS AND ANSWERS

1. Who was ill and about to die? What did Jesus do?

   The centurion's slave was ill and about to die, but Jesus healed him because of his faith. Verses 7:8 and 9

2. Who died? What did Jesus do?

   The widow's son had died, but Jesus had him rise and He brought him back to life. Verses 712 to 15

3. What was the most important thing about the sinful woman?

   The sinful woman was sorry for her sins and by her actions one could see that she had faith and loved a lot. Verses 7:44 to 50

4. How is Luke 7:27 in the New Testament like Malachi 3:1 in the Old Testament?

   The verses state that a messenger was being sent to prepare the way of the Lord.

5. Who acknowledged the righteousness of God and who did not?

   The messengers, John the Baptist and the disciples acknowledged the righteousness of God. The Pharisees and scholars of the law did not. Verses 7:29 and 30

Luke 8

QUESTIONS AND RESPONSES

1. What did Jesus do when He went from one town and village to another?

    When Jesus went from one town to another, He preached and proclaimed the good news. Verse 8:1

2. What were some parables that Jesus taught with?

    Some parables that Jesus taught with were the parable of the sower and the parable of the lamp. Titles prior to Verse 8:4 and Verse 8:16.

3. What were some healings that he did?

    Some of the healings that Jesus did were: the healing of the demoniac, the healing of Jairus' daughter and the healing of the woman with a hemorrhage. Titles prior to Verse 8:26 and Verse 8:40

4. In the parable of the sower, the seed is the _____

    The seed is the "Word of God". Verse 8:15

5. How is the verse Luke 8:31 in the New Testament similar to Genesis 1:2 in the Old Testament?

    Both verses talk about the abyss. The abyss is the place of the dead or the prison of Satan or the chaos before creation.

Luke 9

QUESTIONS AND RESPONSES

1. What did Jesus give to the twelve?

    Jesus gave power and authority over all demons, power to cure diseases and authority to proclaim the kingdom of God. Verses 9:1 and 2

2. How did Jesus pray in this chapter?

    Jesus prayed in solitude (alone). Verse 9:1

3. What did Jesus say in the First Prediction of the Passion?

    In the First Prediction of the Passion, Jesus said: "The Son of Man must suffer greatly and be rejected by the elders, the chief priests, and the scribes and be killed and on the third day be raised." Verse 9:22

4. What did Jesus say in the Second Prediction of the Passion?

    In the Second Prediction of the Passion, Jesus said: "Pay attention to what I am telling you. The Son of Man is to be handed over to men." Verse 9:44

5. How is the verse Luke 9:5 like the verse Matthew 10:14 in the New Testament?

    Both of these verses give the advice that if others do not welcome or listen when you talk about Jesus, to leave them and shake the dust from your feet.

Luke 10

QUESTIONS AND RESPONSES

1. How many did the Lord appoint as followers on a mission?

   The Lord appointed seventy-two followers on a mission. Verse 10:1

2. What is the greatest commandment?

   The greatest commandment is: "You shall love the Lord, your God, with all your heart, with all your being, with all your strength, and with all your mind, and your neighbor as yourself." Verse 10:27

3. How are we to treat our neighbor?

   You are to treat your neighbor with mercy. Verse 10:37

4. What quality of Mary did Jesus point out when Martha was anxious with serving?

   The quality of listening is what Jesus pointed out when Martha was anxious about serving. Verse 10:39

5. How is the verse Matthew 10:13 like Luke 10:5 in the New Testament?

   These verses speak about giving peace to the people you meet.

Luke 11

QUESTIONS AND RESPONSES

1. What prayer did Jesus teach the disciples?

    Jesus taught the disciple the "Our Father". Verses 11:2 through 11:4

2. Jesus said:

    "Ask and you will _____. receive
    Seek and you will _____. find
    Knock and the door will be _____.opened to you
    verse 11:9

3. "Blessed are those who hear the word of God and _____.
    observe it Verse 11:28

4. What did Jesus tell the Pharisees to pay attention to?

    Jesus told the Pharisees to pay attention to God and to judgment. Verses
    11:49-51

5. How is Luke 11:1-4 and Matthew 6:9-13 in the New Testament different
    and similar?

    Both are about "The Lord's Prayer".

Luke 12

QUESTIONS AND RESPONSES

1. What are we to have under persecution?

   We are to have courage under persecution. The title before verse 12:2.

2. Who will help you teach others about Jesus?

   The Holy Spirit will help you teach others about Jesus. Verse 12:12

3. What matters are we to be rich in?

   We are to be rich in the things of heaven. We are to depend on God and live for God. verses 12:31-34

4. We are not to worry or be anxious so what are we to seek?

   We are to seek the kingdom of God. Verse 12:31

5. How is Luke 12:1 like Mark 8:15 in the New Testament?

   We are to be aware of the leaven. The leaven is evil attitudes.

Luke 13

QUESTIONS AND RESPONSES

1. What will happen to those who do not repent? What does repent mean?

    People who do not repent will perish and go to hell. Repent means to be sorry for our sins. Verses 13:2 and 13:3

2. Name at least three parables in this chapter.

    Three parables in this chapter are: the Parable of the Barren Fig Tree, the Parable of the Mustard Seed and the Parable of the Yeast. Titles prior to Verses: 13:6, 13:18 and 13:20.

3. What is meant by the narrow door?

    The narrow door means that great effort and strength are needed to enter heaven. Verse 13:24

4. What did Jesus do on the Sabbath? Why was this a good act?

    Jesus cured the crippled woman on the Sabbath. Jesus had set her free from bondage after eighteen years. Verses 13:13 and 13:16

5. How is Exodus 20:9-10 in the Old Testament like Luke 13:14 in the New Testament?

    Both Bible passages talk about six days of labor being done in a week.

Luke 14

QUESTIONS AND RESPONSES

1. Who was healed on the Sabbath?

    The man with dropsy was healed on the Sabbath. Verse 14:4

2. Who does Jesus recommend to be the invited guests at a banquet?

    Jesus recommends inviting the crippled, the lame and the blind to a banquet. Verse 14:13

3. What was interesting in the parable of the Great Feast?

    In the parable of the Great Feast it was interesting that strangers were invited. Verse 14:23

4. What are some sayings about discipleship?

    Some sayings in regards to discipleship are: carry your cross, make plans and make God the most important. 14:27-33

5. How is Proverbs 25:6 in the Old Testament like Luke 14:8 in the New Testament?

    Both verses state that one should not sit where a more distinguished person might sit.

Luke 15

QUESTIONS AND RESPONSES

1. What are the three parables in this chapter?

    Three parables in this chapter are: The Parable of the Lost Sheep, the Parable of the Lost Coin and the Parable of the Lost Son, Titles prior to verses 15:1, 15:8 and 15:11.

2. What are we to do when a sinner repents?

    When a sinner repents, we are to rejoice. verse 15:7

3. What did the scribes and Pharisees complain about?

    The scribes and Pharisees complained about Jesus welcoming sinners and eating with sinners. Verse 15:2

4. What do the parables in this chapter teach us?

    The parables in this chapter teach of Jesus' great concern for those who are lost. He has love for the repentant sinner. Verses 15:6 and 15:7

5. How is Proverbs 18:24 in the Old Testament like Luke 15:32 in the New Testament?

    They both speak of love for ones brother.

Luke 16

QUESTIONS AND RESPONSES

1. What is a teaching about honesty?

    The person who is trustworthy in small matters is also trustworthy in great matters. Verse 16:10

2. What is a saying against the Pharisees in regards to money?

    You justify yourselves in the sight of others, but God knows your heart. Verse 16:15

3. Who was the poor man in the parable?

    The poor man in this chapter is Lazarus. Verse 16:20

4. Do you think it is bad to be rich?

    PERSONAL THOUGHTS AND/OR FEELINGS

5. How is Matthew 6:24 in the New Testament like Luke 16:13 in the New Testament?

    Both mention that no one can serve two masters because one will be loved and one will be hated.

Luke 17

QUESTIONS AND RESPONSES

1. What are we to do if our brother sins?

    If our brother sins we are to rebuke him, but if he repents we are to forgive him. Verse 17:3

2. What did the apostles say to the Lord?

    The apostles asked the Lord to increase their faith. Verse 17:5

3. What did one of the ten lepers that were cleansed do?

    One of the ten lepers glorified Jesus and thanked Him for being cleansed. Verses 17:15 and 17:16

4. What did Jesus say to the foreigner who returned to give thanks?

    Jesus said to the foreigner: "Ten were cleansed, were they not? Where are the other nine? Has none but this foreigner returned to give thanks?" Verses 17:17 and 17:18

5. How is Genesis 6:8 in the Old Testament like Luke 17:26 in the New Testament?

    Both verses are about Noah and the Lord.

Luke 18

QUESTIONS AND RESPONSES

1. What helped the judge to deliver a just decision?

    The widow who kept bothering the judge helped him to make a just decision because he feared she might come and strike him. verse 18:4

2. What does it mean to be humble?

    To be humble means to not brag about one's good deeds, but to always be open to doing good and to doing better. verse 18:14

3. How did Jesus respond to children?

    Jesus said: "Let the children come to me and do not prevent them; for the kingdom of God belongs to such as these." verse 18:16

4. What saved the blind man?

    The blind man regained his sight and because of his faith Jesus healed him, verse 18:43

5. How is Exodus 20:12-17 in the Old Testament like Luke 18:20 in the New Testament?

    The Ten Commandments are in these passages.

Luke 19

QUESTIONS AND RESPONSES

1. What lesson can we learn from Zacchaeus?

    From Zacchaeus we can learn to try to see Jesus' works in our everyday life and to be willing to make up for the things we do not do that we should do. Verse 19:8

2. What lesson can we learn from the parable of the ten gold coins?

    From the parable of the ten coins we can learn to be good and productive servants of the Lord and to listen carefully to the Word. Verse Luke 19:11-27 note

3. On what day in the Church year do we celebrate the Entry into Jerusalem?

    We celebrate the Entry into Jerusalem (19:28) on Palm Sunday each year. Verse John 12:13 note

4. What kind of house does Jesus expect the temple to be?

    Jesus expects the Temple to be a House of Prayer. verse 19:46

5. How is the verse in Malachi 3:1 of the Old Testament like the verse in Luke 19:38 of the New Testament?

    Both are about the one who comes, Jesus.

Luke 20

QUESTIONS AND RESPONSES

1. Who questioned the authority of Jesus?

    The authority of Jesus was questioned by chief priests, scribes and the elders. Verse 20:1 and 20:2

2. What was a lesson from the parable of the tenant farmers?

    A lesson of respect is in this parable. verse 20:13

3. Why was Jesus being asked questions about the taxes to the Emperor?

    Jesus was being asked questions about the taxes to the Emperor as a way to force Him to take sides on sensitive political issues. Verse 20:26

4. Why was Jesus being asked questions about the Resurrection?

    Some of the Sadducees did not believe in the Resurrection. verse 20:27

5. How is Psalm 110:1 in the Old Testament like Luke 20:42-43 in the New Testament?

    They both state: "The Lord said to my Lord, sit at my right hand till I make your enemies your footstool."

Luke 21

QUESTIONS AND RESPONSES

1. Why was the widow's contribution so great?

    The widow offered her whole livelihood, all that she had. Verse 21:4

2. What did you find interesting about the end times?

    The end times are to have signs like false prophets, earthquakes, nations fighting against nations, famines, plagues, sights and signs from the sky. Verses 21:10 and 21:11

3. What does persecution mean?

    Persecution is being hated by others because of your love for Jesus. Verse 21:17

4. What will help us to escape tribulations?

    We will be helped to escape this tribulation by praying to have the strength and by standing before the Son of Man. Verse 21:36

5. How is 2 Chronicles 15:6 in the Old Testament like Luke 21:10 in the New Testament?

    Both passages speak of nations against other nations and nations crushing other nations.

Luke 22

QUESTIONS AND RESPONSES

1. When was the institution of the Eucharist?

    The institution of the Eucharist was at the Last Supper. verses 22:14-20

2. What was Peter's denial about?

    Peter denied Jesus three times and then the cock crowed as Jesus had told them that this would happen. Verses 22:54-61

3. What was the Agony in the Garden about?

    Jesus was in the garden and He asked His disciples to pray as well. He prayed so hard that His sweat was like drops of blood. Then He found the disciples sleeping and told them to get up and pray. Verses 22:40-46

4. What was the Betrayal and Arrest of Jesus about?

    Judas betrayed Jesus. Someone cut off the ear of a high priest and Jesus healed it, but the guards and chief priests came to arrest Him. Verses 22:48-53

5. How is Zechariah 9:11 in the Old Testament like Luke 22:20 in the New Testament?

    The similar words are blood and covenant.

Luke 23

1. What did Pilate tell the chief priests and the crowds at first?

    Pilate told the chief priests and crowds: "I find this man not guilty." Verse 23:4

2. Who did Pilate become friends with?

    Pilate became friends with Herod. verse 23:12

3. What did the crowds keep yelling at Pilate?

    The crowds kept yelling at Pilate: "Crucify Him!" verse 23:21

4. When Jesus was crucified, who was on His right and His left?

    When Jesus was crucified, a criminal on the right and a criminal on the left were also there. Verse 23:33

5. How is Psalm 22:19 in the Old Testament like Luke 23:34 in the New Testament?

    Both verses are about dividing the garments and casting lots.

Luke 24

QUESTIONS AND RESPONSES

1. How many days after the crucifixion did Jesus rise from the dead? Who was at the tomb to find this out?

    After the crucifixion, Jesus rose from the dead three days later. Mary Magdalene, Joanna and Mary, the mother of Jesus were at the tomb. Verse 24:7 and verse 24:10

2. What happened on the Road to Emmaus?

    On the Road to Emmaus, Cleopas and his friend were discussing the happenings of the crucifixion and Jesus began to walk with them and asking them about the events, but not until they ate and broke the Bread did they recognize Him, Verses 24:17-31

3. What happened when Jesus appeared to the disciples after His Resurrection?

    When Jesus appeared to the disciples, they were startled and terrified. Verse 24:37

4. What was the Ascension like?

    At the Ascension, Jesus raised His hands, blest them, departed from them and was taken up to heaven. Verses 24:50 and 24:51

5. How is Isaiah 53:3 in the Old Testament like Luke 24:26 in the New Testament?

    Both verses are about suffering.

John 1

QUESTIONS AND RESPONSES

1. The Gospel of John contains a lot of wondrous deeds. These are also called, what?

   The wondrous deeds in the Gospel of John are called "signs". Introduction notes on the Gospel of John.

2. Who was one of the first people to give testimony of Jesus?

   One of the first people to give testimony of Jesus was John the Baptist. Verses 1:29-32.

3. In what location was John the Baptist baptizing?

   John was baptizing in Bethany across the Jordan Verse 1:28

4. The Holy Spirit is often said to come down like a _____. (dove) What does this mean?

   The dove is a symbol of a new creation. verse 1:33

5. Who were three of the first disciples of Jesus?

   The three first disciples were: Andrew, John and Simon Peter. Verses 1:35-40

6. What symbol is there for "under the fig tree"? How is Micah 4:4 like John 1:48?

   The symbol for "under the fig tree" is messianic peace. Note of verse 48. Both verses state: "under the fig tree".

John 2

QUESTIONS AND RESPONSES

1. What was the first sign at the beginning of the ministry of Jesus?

   The first sign at the beginning of the ministry of Jesus was when He changed the water into wine at the Wedding of Cana. Verse 2:3-11

2. Who were the people present at the beginning of the ministry of Jesus?

   The people present at the beginning of the ministry of Jesus were the mother of Jesus, the disciples, the head waiter and the servers. Verses 2:1-12

3. Where did this event take place?

   The event took place at Cana in Galilee. Verse 2:11

4. What event took place that brought significance to the Resurrection?

   The event that took place that brought significance to the Resurrection was the cleansing of the temple. Verses 2:14-22

5. Who was present at this event and what animals were present?

   Sellers and money changers were in the temple as well as oxen, sheep and doves. Verse 2:14

6. How is Hosea 6:2 in the Old Testament like John 2:19 in the New Testament?

   Both passages are about on the third day of being raised up.

John 3

QUESTIONS AND RESPONSES

1. Who was Nicodemus?

    Nicodemus is a Pharisee, a ruler of the Jews. verse 3:1

2. What did God give because of his love for the world?

    Because of His love for the world, God gave His Son, Jesus. verse 3:16

3. What was the purpose of Jesus?

    Jesus came to save the world. Verse 3:17

4. What are we to do to have eternal life?

    To have eternal life we are to believe In Jesus and His works. verse 3:15

5. Who hates the light?

    People who do evil hate the light. Verse 3:20

6. Who comes to the light?

    Whoever lives the truth comes to the light, so that his works may be clearly seen as done in God. Verse 3:21

John 4

QUESTIONS AND RESPONSES

1. Who did Jesus talk to from Judea to Galilee and what did they talk about?

    On the way to Galilee Jesus talked to His disciples and the Samaritan woman. They talked about the gift of God and eternal life. Verses 4:4-27

2. What place was this and whose land was nearby?

    This place was Samaria. This was Jacob's land that he gave to his son, Joseph. Verse 4:5

3. How are people to worship?

    People are to worship in Spirit and in truth. Verse 4:23

4. How long did Jesus stay in Samaria? Why?

    Jesus stayed in Samaria for two days because a prophet has no honor in his native land. Verse 4:44

5. What was the second sign that Jesus performed in Galilee?

    The second sign that Jesus performed in Galilee was the cure of a royal official's son in Capernaum. Verses 4:46-50

6. How is Deuteronomy 18:15 in the Old Testament like John 4:25 in the New Testament?

    Both verses are about the great prophet.

John 5

QUESTIONS AND RESPONSE

1. What was the cure on the Sabbath and where did it take place?

   The cure on the Sabbath was of a man who was born ill and continued ill for 38 years. This was in Jerusalem at the Sheep (Gate) a pool called Bethesda in Hebrew. Verses 5:1-9

2. Why did the Jews try to kill Jesus?

   The Jews tried to kill Jesus because He cured on the Sabbath. verses 5:10-18

3. Who has eternal life?

   Whoever hears the Word and believes in the One who sent Jesus. verse 5: 24

4. What justifies Jesus doing what his Father does?

   Jesus dependence on the Father is justification for doing what the Father does. The note of verse 5:19

5. Whose testimony is greater than John's?

   Jesus' testimony is greater than John's. verse 5:36

6. How is 1 Samuel 2:6 in the Old Testament like John 5:21 in the New Testament?

   Both verses are about the Lord who gives life.

John 6

QUESTIONS AND RESPONSE

1. Why did the large crowd follow Jesus when He went across the Sea of Galilee?

   The large crowd followed Jesus when He went across the Sea of Galilee because of the signs that they saw Him performing on the sick. Verse 6:2

2. Why did the disciples become afraid when they were in the boat and had rowed out about three or four miles on the sea to Capernaum?

   The disciples were afraid when they were on the boat because it was dark and strong winds began to blow. Verses 6:17 and 6:18

3. Who will not reject anyone who comes to Him?

   Jesus will not reject anyone who comes to him. Verse 6:37

4. What is the spirit of life?

   The spirit of life is the words spoken by Jesus. Verse 6:63

5. Who betrayed Jesus? Whose son was he?

   Judas betrayed Jesus. Judas was the son of Simon, the Iscariot. Verse 6:71

6. How is the verse Psalm 78:24 like the verse John 6:31?

   Both verses are about bread from heaven.

John 7

QUESTIONS AND RESPONSE

1. Why did Jesus just move around within Galilee rather than travel to Judea?

   Jesus moved around in Galilee rather than travel in Judea because the Jews were trying to kill Him. Verse 7:1

2. Who are the people that are truthful?

   The people that are truthful are those who seek the glory of God, the Father. Verse 7:18

3. Who sent guards to arrest Jesus?

   The chief priests and Pharisees sent guards to arrest Jesus. Verse 7:32

4. What is meant by living water?

   Living water is the gift of the Holy Spirit. verses 7:38 and 7:39

5. What was the discussion on concerning where the Messiah would come from?

   There was a discussion on whether the Messiah would come from Galilee or from Bethlehem, the village where David lived, Verses 7:41 and 7:42

6. How is the verse Exodus 17:6 in the Old Testament like the verse John 7:38 in the New Testament?

   Both verses say: "the water will flow ".

John 8

QUESTIONS AND RESPONSE

1. What was Jesus doing in the temple area in the morning?

   Jesus was teaching the people in the temple area. Verse 8:2

2. What will people have if they follow Jesus?

   The people that follow Jesus will have the light of life. verse 8:12

3. What did Jesus tell the Jews about how they would be if they believed in Him?

   Jesus said: "If you remain in my word, you will truly be my disciples." Verse 8:31

4. Who were the people who asked Jesus if He was possessed?

   The Jews asked Jesus if He was possessed. Verses 8:48 and 8:49

5. What did Jesus do when the Jews picked up stones to throw at Him?

   When the Jews picked up stones and threw them at Him, He went out of the temple area and hid. Verse 8:59

6. How is the verse of John 8:7 in the New Testament like Deuteronomy 17:7 in the Old Testament?

   Both are about the first witnesses of evil.

John 9

QUESTIONS AND RESPONSE

1. What was Jesus response when the disciples asked Him who sinned when they saw a blind man, the blind man or his parents?

   When the disciples asked Jesus who sinned, if it was the blind man or his parents, Jesus replied that neither had sinned. Verses 9:2 and 9:3

2. What was the response of the blind man when others asked him how his eyes were opened?

   When the Pharisees asked the blind man how his eyes were opened, he said; "Jesus put clay on my eyes, and then I washed and now I can see." Verse 9:15

3. What was the response of the blind man when the Pharisees asked him, "What do you have to say about him, since he opened your eyes?"

   The blind man responded that Jesus is a prophet. Verse 9:17

4. What answer did the parents give when asked the question by the Jews, "How does your son see now?" When the Jews asked the parents about how their son can see now, they responded:

   "We do not know how he sees, nor do we know who opened his eyes. Ask him, he is of age, he can speak for himself." Verse 9:21

5. What was one of the rules of Jewish Tradition that the Pharisees said Jesus had broken?

   The rule of the Jewish Tradition that Jesus had broken was not to cure on the Sabbath. Verse 9:14

6. How is Exodus 20:5 in the Old Testament like the verse in the New Testament, John 9:2?

Both verses are about a parent's sins that are passed on.

John 10

QUESTIONS AND RESPONSE

1. Why did Jesus come?

    Jesus came so people may have life and have it more abundantly. verse 10:10

2. What does a good shepherd do?

    A good shepherd lays down his life for his sheep. Verse 10:11

3. What does a good shepherd know?

    A good shepherd knows his sheep. verse 10:14

4. What was the Feast of Dedication?

    The Feast of Dedication was an eight day festival of lights held in December to celebrate the Maccabees' rededication of the altar and reconsecration of the temple. This was in Jerusalem and it was a Hebrew celebration. Notes from verse 10:22

5. What did Jesus tell the Jews to believe, if they did not believe in Him?

    Jesus told the Jews to believe His works so that they might realize and understand that the Father is in Me and I am in the Father. Verse 10:38

6. How is the verse Psalm 80:2 in the Old Testament like John 10:2 in the New Testament?

    Both verses are about the shepherd of the flock,

John 11

QUESTIONS AND RESPONSE

1. What did Jesus do for Martha and Mary and the crowd?

    Jesus raised Lazarus from the dead for this was the brother of Martha and Mary of Bethany. Verse 11:1

2. Why did Jesus perform this miracle?

    Jesus performed this miracle so that people would believe that He is Jesus and was sent by the Father. Verses 11:41 and 11:42

3. Who came to believe in Jesus because of this miracle?

    Because of this miracle many Jews came to believe in Jesus. verse 11:45

4. What kind of plan did the Pharisees begin to make?

    The Pharisees began to make plans to kill Jesus. verse 11:53

5. Where did Jesus go and who was He with?

    Jesus went with his disciples to the town of Ephraim near a desert. verse 11:54

6. How are the verses Exodus 19:10-11 in the Old Testament like John 11:55 in the New Testament?

    Both verses are about purifying and washing oneself.

John 12

QUESTIONS AND RESPONSE

1. Why did a large crowd of Jews and the chief priests come to Bethany where Lazarus was?

   The large crowd of Jews and chief priests came to Bethany to see Jesus and Lazarus whom He had raised from the dead. Verse 12:9

2. Why were palm branches used to welcome Jesus?

   Palm branches at that time were used to welcome great conquerors. Note from verse 12:13

3. What feast were the people gathering for?

   The people were gathering for the Feast of Tabernacles.
   Note from verse 12:13

4. Who is the ruler of the world that will be driven out?

   Satan is a ruler of the world that will be thrown out. Note from Verse 12:31

5. If we believe in Jesus, who must we also believe in?

   If we believe in Jesus, we also must believe in the one who sent Him, God the Father, Verses 12:44 and 12:45

6. How is the verse 1 Maccabees 13:51 in the Old Testament like John 12:13 in the New Testament?

   Both verses are about palm branches.

John 13

QUESTIONS AND RESPONSE

1. When Jesus washed the feet of the disciples, what was He teaching us?

    When Jesus washed the feet of the disciples, He was teaching us to be servants and that we need to be cleansed of our sins. Notes from Verses 13:1-20

2. When and why was Jesus deeply troubled?

    Jesus was deeply troubled after the washing of the disciples' feet because He knew Judas was going to betray Him. Verses 13:21-28

3. What was the new commandment that Jesus gave to us?

    The new commandment that Jesus gave was: "Love one another. As I have loved you, so you also should love one another." Verse 13:34

4. Who would deny Jesus three times?

    Peter denied Jesus three times. Verse 13:38

5. What was the sign or signal that someone had denied Jesus three times?

    The sign or the signal that someone had denied Jesus three times was the cock that crowed. Verse 13:38

6. How is the verse Leviticus 19:18 in the Old Testament like John 13:34 in the New Testament?

    Both verses are about loving another and loving your neighbor.

John 14

QUESTIONS AND RESPONSES

1. What will the believers of Jesus do?

   Believers will do the works that Jesus does and even greater ones. So believers are to ask the Father in Jesus name and it will be done. Verses 14:12-14

2. Who are we to have faith in?

   We are to have faith in Jesus and believe that Jesus is in the Father. Verse 14:11

3. If we love Jesus and keep His commandments, what will the Father give us to be with us always?

   If we keep the commandments, the Father will give us the Spirit of truth to be with us always. Verses 14:16 and 14:17

4. How are we to come to the Father?

   We are to come to the Father with love for Jesus by keeping His Word. Verse 14:23

5. If Jesus says our hearts are not to be troubled or afraid, then what are they to be?

   Our hearts are to be rejoicing. Verse 14:28

6. How is Wisdom 6:18 in the Old Testament like John 14:15 in the New Testament?

   Both verses are about love. Love is keeping the commandments.

John 15

QUESTIONS AND RESPONSES

1. Who is the vine and who is the vine grower?

    The vine is Jesus. The vine grower is the Father. verse 15:1

2. How can we bear fruit?

    We can bear fruit by remaining in Jesus and His Word and keep the commandments. Verses 15:4-10

3. Why were we given the command to love one another?

    We were given the command to love one another so we may have complete joy. verse 15:11

4. Who is our Advocate?

    Our advocate is the Spirit of truth. verse 15:26

5. Who was hated by the world first?

    Jesus was hated by the world first. verse 15:18

6. How is verse Psalm 69:5 in the Old Testament like John 15:25 in the New Testament?

    Both verses are about hate without cause.

John 16

QUESTIONS AND RESPONSE

1. Who will guide us to all truth?

    The Advocate, the spirit, will guide us to all truth. verse 16:13

2. Why are we to ask the Father for things in Jesus' name?

    We are to ask the Father for things in Jesus name so that our joy may be complete. Verse 16:24

3. When we have trouble in this world, why are we to have courage?

    When we have trouble in this world, we are to have courage because Jesus has conquered the world so that we may have peace. Verse 16:33

4. How has the ruler of the world been condemned?

    The ruler of the world has been condemned because of Jesus' death. Notes of Verses 16:8-11

5. Who realized that they did not need to question Jesus anymore?

    The disciples realized that they did not need to question Jesus anymore. Verse 16:30

6. How is the verse Jeremiah 31:13 in the Old Testament like John 16:20 in the New Testament?

    They are about how mourning will be turned to joy.

John 17

QUESTIONS AND RESPONSE

1. What was Jesus doing when he raised His eyes to heaven and spoke?

   When Jesus raised His eyes to heaven and spoke, He was praying the "high priestly prayer" of Jesus. Note of Verses 17:1-26

2. What did it sound like to you? What lesson or meaning did you get?

   PERSONAL THOUGHTS AND/OR FEELINGS

3. What kind of things did Jesus ask the Father for?

   Jesus asked the Father that all people may be One with Him and the Father and to be kept from the evil one. Verses 17:11 and 17:15

4. What does Jesus wish for us?

   Jesus wants us to believe in Him and that He was sent by the Father and is One with the Father. Verses 17:20 and 17:21

5. What does Jesus make known to us from the Father?

   Jesus makes known to the Father that we are gifts. Verse 17:24

6. How is the verse Wisdom 15:3 in the Old Testament like John 17:26 in the New Testament?

   Both verses are about coming to know one.

John 18

QUESTIONS AND RESPONSE

1. What may have been symbolic of the hour of darkness?

    Lanterns and torches may have been symbolic of the hour of darkness. Notes from Verse 18:3

2. Who asked Peter if he was one of Jesus' disciples?

    The maid, the gate keeper, asked Peter if he was one of Jesus' disciples. Verse 18:17

3. Who questioned Jesus about his disciples and doctrine?

    The high priest questioned Jesus about the disciples and doctrine. Verse 18:19

4. What questions did Pilate ask Jesus?

    Pilates asked Jesus: "Are You King of the Jews? What have you done?" Verses 18:33 and 18:35

5. What was the custom at Passover?

    The custom of the Passover was to eat a meal and to release one prisoner. Verses 18:28 and 18:39

6. What is in verse 2 Samuel 15:23 of the Old Testament that is like John 18:12 of the New Testament?

    These verses are about soldiers.

John 19

QUESTIONS AND RESPONSE

1. What did Pilate have the soldiers do?

    Pilate had the soldiers scourge Jesus, put a crown of thorns on his head and clothed Him in a purple cloak. Verses 19:1 and 19:2

2. What did the chief priests and guards cry out when they saw Jesus?

    When the chief priests and guards saw Jesus, they cried out: "Crucify him, Crucify him." Verse 19:6

3. Where and with whom was Jesus crucified?

    Jesus was crucified with two others one on each side at the Place of the Skull, Golgotha. Verses: 19:17 and 19:18

4. What did the inscription say that was written on the cross?

    The inscription that was written on the cross said: "Jesus the Nazorean, the King of the Jews." Verse 19:19

5. Why were the bodies not to remain on the cross?

    The bodies were not to remain on the cross because it was preparation day and bodies were not to remain on the cross on the Sabbath. Verse 19:31

6. How is the verse Psalm 22:19 in the Old Testament like John 19:24 in the New Testament?

    Both verses are about dividing garments and casting lots.

John 20

QUESTIONS AND RESPONSE

1.   When did Mary and Magdala go to the tomb?

     Mary and Magdala went to the tomb on the first day early in the morning.
     Verse 20:1

2.   What did Jesus tell Mary when she was weeping at the tomb?

     When Mary was weeping at the tomb, Jesus told her: "Woman, why are
     you weeping? Whom are you looking for?" Verse 20:15

3.   Where and when did Jesus appear to his disciples? What did He say to them?

     Jesus appeared to his disciples in Jerusalem on the evening of the first day
     of the week and said to them: "Peace be with you." Verse 20:19

4.   What disciple was not there when Jesus appeared? What did Jesus say to
     him when he appeared again?

     The disciple that was not there when Jesus appeared was Thomas. When
     Jesus appeared again, He said to Thomas: "Peace be with you. Put your
     finger here and see my hands, and bring your hand and put it into my side,
     and do not be unbelieving, but believe." Verses 20:24, 20:26 and 20:27

5.   What has been written so that we might come to believe?

     What has been written so that we might believe is that Jesus is the Messiah, the
     Son of God, and through this belief, we might have life in His name. Verse 20:31

6.   How is the verse Psalm 22:17 in the Old Testament like John 20:20 in the New?

     The Old Testament is about hands and feet and the New is about hands
     and side.

John 21

QUESTIONS AND RESPONSE

1. Where and to what seven disciples did Jesus reveal Himself?

   Jesus revealed Himself at the Sea of Tiberias to Simon Peter, Thomas, Nathanael, Zebedee's sons and two other disciples. Verses 21:1 and 21:2

2. What happened when Jesus told them to cast the net over the right side of the boat?

   When Jesus told the children to cast the net over the right side of the boat, it became so full that they were not able to pull it because it was so full. Verses 21:5 and 21:6

3. What did Peter and Jesus discuss?

   Peter and Jesus discussed whether Peter loved Jesus or not. verses 21:15-21:18

4. What do the words "until I come" mean?

   The words "until I come" are referring to Parousia or heaven. Note of Verse 21:22

5. Why could one not describe all the things Jesus did??

   The whole world could not contain all of these books. Verse 21:25

6. How is the verse Ezekial 47:10 in the Old Testament like John 21:11 in the New Testament?

   These verses are about a lot of fish.

Acts of the Apostles 1

QUESTIONS AND RESPONSES

1. How are we baptized? How did John baptize?

    We are baptized with the Holy Spirit. John baptized with water. verse 1:5

2. What do we call: Jesus being taken up to heaven?

    We call the event of Jesus being taken up to heaven "the Ascension". The title before Verse 1:6 and Verse 1:9

3. Who devoted themselves with one accord in prayer?

    The apostles, some women and Mary, the mother of Jesus devoted themselves with one accord in prayer. Verses 1:13 and 1:14

4. Who was chosen to take the place of Judas?

    Matthias was chosen to take the place of Judas. Verse 1:26

5. What was an important thing that the disciples did when selecting Judas replacement?

    The important thing that the disciples did when replacing Judas was that they prayed about it. Verse 1:24

6. How is Deuteronomy 8:2 in the Old Testament like Acts of the Apostles 1:3 in the New Testament?

    Both verses are about forty. (forty years and forty days)

Acts of the Apostles 2

QUESTIONS AND RESPONSES

1. What was it like when the time for Pentecost was fulfilled?

   When the time for Pentecost was fulfilled all the apostles were together and a noise like a strong wind filled the house. Verse 2:1 and 2:2

2. Who were the people staying in Jerusalem at this time?

   The people that were staying in Jerusalem at this time were the Jews from every nation. Verse 2:5

3. Why were those people confused?

   People were confused because of the different languages being spoken. Verse 2:6

4. What did Peter tell the Israelites to do?

   Peter told the Israelites to repent and be baptized. Verse 2:38

5. What did the apostles devote themselves to everyday?

   Every day the apostles devoted themselves to meeting together in the temple area and to breaking bread in their homes. Verse 2:42 or 2:46

6. How is Exodus 19:18 of the Old Testament like Acts of the Apostles 2:3 in the New Testament?

   Both verses focus on the word, fire.

Acts of the Apostles 3

QUESTIONS AND RESPONSES

1. What time did Peter and John go to the temple area to pray?

   Peter and John went to the temple area at three o'clock to pray. verse 3:1

2. What did Peter do for the crippled beggar?

   Peter cured the crippled beggar. Verses 3:6 and 3:7

3. What were the first things the crippled man did after their encounter?

   The first things the crippled man did was: leaped up, stood, and walked around and went into the temple with them, walking, jumping and praising God. Verse 3:8

4. Who is called the "author of life".

   Jesus is called the "author of life". verse 3:15

5. What was it that the crippled beggar had that made him perfect?

   The crippled beggar had faith and this is what made him Perfect. verse 3:16

6. How is Deuteronomy 18:15 in the Old Testament like Acts of the Apostles 3:22 in the New Testament?

   Both verses state: "A prophet like me will the Lord, your God, raise up for you from you among your own kinsmen; to him you shall listen."

Acts of the Apostles 4

QUESTIONS AND RESPONSES

1. What happened to those who came to hear the Word?

    Those who came to hear the Word came to believe. Verse 4:4

2. Who is the stone that was rejected?

    The stone that was rejected was Jesus Christ, the Nazorean. verses 4:10 and 4:11

3. How was Peter and John described?

    Peter and John were described as bold, uneducated and ordinary. Verse 4:13

4. How did the chief priests and elders pray?

    The chief priests and elders prayed with one accord. They raised their voices and prayed. Verses 4:23 and 4:24

5. What was life like in the Christian Community?

    Life in the Christian Community was a people of believers of one heart and mind, and no one claimed that any of his possessions was his own. Verse 4:32

6. How is Exodus 19:18 of the Old Testament like Acts of the Apostles 4:31 in the New Testament?

    In the Old Testament the mountains trembled and in the New Testament the place shook at prayer time.

Acts of the Apostles 5

QUESTIONS AND RESPONSES

1. What was the sin of Ananias and Sapphira?

    The sin of Ananias and Sapphira was a lie. Verse 5:3 and 5:4

2. What were some of the signs and wonders performed by the apostles?

    Some of the signs and wonders performed by the apostles was the curing of the sick and the curing of those disturbed by unclean spirits. Verse 4:16

3. What did the high priests and Sadducees do to the apostles? Why?

    The high priests and Sadducees laid hands on the apostles and put them in jail because they were jealous of them. Verses 4:17 and 4:18

4. What happened to the apostles during the night?

    During the night the apostles were let out of prison by an angel and were told to go to the temple area. Verses 4:19 and 4:20

5. A Pharisee in the Sanhedrin, Gamaliel, gave what advice to the Israelites?

    A Pharisee in the Sanhedrin, Gamaliel, advised the Israelites to be careful of what they do to these apostles. Verse 4:35

6. How is Deuteronomy 13:5 in the Old Testament like Acts of the Apostles 5:29 in the New Testament?

    Both are about observing the commandments rather than man.

Acts of the Apostles 6

QUESTIONS AND RESPONSES

1. What were seven men to be devoted to?

   Seven men were devoted to the care of the needy. Verse 6:1

2. What is another name for those seven assistants?

   Deacon is another name for the seven assistants.

3. Who was working great wonders and signs among the people?

   Stephen was working wonders and signs among the people. Verse 6:8

4. What were the essential functions of the twelve apostles?

   The essential functions of the twelve apostles were prayer and the service of the Word. Verse 6:4

5. What is the customary Jewish way of designating persons for a task and invoking upon them the divine blessing and power to perform it?

   The Jewish customary way of designating a person for tasks and invoking on them the divine blessing and power to perform it was laying hands on them and praying. Verse 6:6

6. How is Exodus 20:21 in the Old Testament like the verse in the New Testament Acts of the Apostles 6:14?

   They are about Moses and the people.

Acts of the Apostles 7

QUESTIONS AND RESPONSES

1. Who sold Joseph into slavery in Egypt?

    The patriarchs sold Joseph into slavery. verse 7:9

2. How was Moses educated?

    Moses was educated in all wisdom of the Egyptians and was powerful in his words and deeds. Verse 7:22

3. Where and how did an angel appear to Moses?

    An angel appeared to Moses in the desert near Mount Sinai in the flame of a burning bush. Verse 7:30

4. What happened to Stephen?

    Stephen was stoned to death. Verses 7:58 and 7:59

5. What were the last words of Stephen?

    The last words of Stephen were: "Lord Jesus, receive my spirit". Verse 7:59

6. How is Exodus 1:5 in the Old Testament like Acts of the Apostles 7:9 in the New Testament?

    These verses are about Joseph in Egypt.

Acts of the Apostles 8

QUESTIONS AND RESPONSES

1. Where was the persecution of the church taking place?

    The persecution of the church was taking place in Jerusalem. verse 8:1

2. What were some of the signs performed by Phillip?

    Some of the signs performed by Philip were: the curing of crippled and paralyzed people and unclean spirits coming out of possessed people. Verse 8:7

3. What did Simon do before he was baptized by Phillip?

    Before Simon was baptized, he practiced magic. Verse 8:9

4. The angel of the Lord spoke to Phillip and where was he told to go?

    The angel told Phillip to go South on the road that goes down from Jerusalem to Gaza, the desert route. Verse 8:26

5. Why did Phillip and the eunuch go down into the water?

    Phillip and the eunuch went into the water so Phillip could baptize him, Verse 8:38

6. How is Isaiah 53:7 in the Old Testament like Acts of the Apostle 8:32 in the New Testament?

    Both verses are about sheep.

Acts of the Apostles 9

QUESTIONS AND RESPONSES

1. What happened to Saul on his way to Damascus?

   On his way to Damascus Saul fell to the ground after a light flashed in front of him and he became blind. Verses 9:4-8

2. What did the disciple, Ananias do for Saul?

   The disciple, Ananias, cured Saul's blindness. verse 9:17

3. What happened to Saul in Jerusalem?

   The Jews tried to kill Saul in Jerusalem. verse 9:23

4. In what countries was the church at peace?

   The countries where the church was at peace were: Judea, Galilee and Samaria. Verse 9:31

5. Who did Peter heal?

   Peter healed Aeneas who was paralyzed and had been confined to bed for eight years. Verse 9:33

6. How is Psalm 2:7 in the Old Testament like Acts of the Apostle 9:20 in the New Testament?

   Both verses are about proclaiming the Lord.

Acts of the Apostles 10

QUESTIONS AND RESPONSES

1. What was the vision of Cornelius?

    The vision of Cornelius was when the angel came to him and said: "Your prayers and almsgiving have ascended as a memorial offering before God. Now send some men to Joppa and summon one Simon who is Peter." Verses 10:4 and 10:5

2. What was the vision of Peter?

    The vision of Peter in a voice was: "What God has made clean, you are not to call profane." verse 10:15

3. In the Bible, what was often used as a number of days?

    In the Bible the number "three" was often used as a number of days. Verse 10:40

4. What time in the afternoon did a lot of things happen in the New Testament?

    A lot of things in the New Testament happened at three o'clock in the afternoon. Verse 10:3 or verse 10:30

5. Who said: "In truth, I see that God shows no partiality"?

    Peter stated: "In truth I show no partiality." Verse 10:34

6. How is Wisdom 6:7 in the Old Testament like Acts of the Apostles 10:34 in the New Testament?

    Both state how the Lord shows no partiality.

Acts of the Apostles 11

QUESTIONS AND RESPONSES

1. What group came to accept the word of God and be baptized?

    The Gentiles came to accept the Word of God and be baptized. Verses 11:1 and 11:16

2. At what place were the first disciples called Christians?

    The first disciples were called Christians at Antioch. verse 11:20

3. Who were the two disciples that taught a large number of people and met for a whole year?

    The two disciples who taught a large number of people and met for a whole year were Barnabas and Saul. Verses 11:22-26

4. Who was the prophet from Jerusalem who predicted a severe famine?

    Agabus was a prophet from Jerusalem who predicted a severe famine. Verse11:28

5. In the Jewish community certain people were referred to as elders or?

    Another word for elders in the Jewish community was presbyters. Verse 11:30

6. How is James 5:14 in the New Testament like Acts of the Apostles 11:30 in the new Testament?

    Both verses are about presbyters.

Acts of the Apostles 12

QUESTIONS AND RESPONSES

1. What did Herod do on the Feast of the Unleavened Bread?

    On the Feast of the Unleavened Bread Herod had James killed and Peter arrested. Verses 12:2 and 12:4

2. What did the angel do for Peter when he was in prison?

    The angel took Peter out of jail. verses 12:6-10

3. What was happening at the house of Mary, the mother of John?

    People were praying at the house of Mary, the mother of John. verse 12:12

4. What did Herod do when he found Peter missing from prison?

    When Herod found Peter missing from prison, he instituted a search, ordered the guards to be tried and executed them and then went to Caesarea. Verse 12:19

5. What was the death of Herod like?

    The death of Herod was when the angel of the Lord struck him down because he did not honor God and then he was eaten by worms and breathed his last. verse 12:23

6. How is 2 Kings 19:35 in the Old Testament like Acts of the Apostles 12:23 in the New Testament?

    Both verses are about the angel of the Lord having struck down someone.

Acts of the Apostles 13

QUESTIONS AND RESPONSES

1. What happened on the first mission of Saul and Barnabas in Cyprus?

    On the first mission of Saul and Barnabas they met a false prophet, a magician, Bar-Jesus. He went blind by the hand of the Lord and then became a believer. Verses 13:6-12

2. What happened at the synagogue in Antioch?

    At the synagogue in Antioch the law and the prophets were read. Verse 13:15

3. Who are two of the prophets that Paul was talking about?

    Paul was talking about the prophet, Samuel and the prophet, David. Verses 13:21 and 13:22

4. Who were some of the people that followed Paul and Barnabas?

    Some of the people who followed Paul and Barnabas were Jews and worshippers who were converts. Verse 13:43

5. What did some of the Jews do when Paul and Barnabas spoke the word of God to the Gentiles?

    When Paul and Barnabas spoke the Word of God to the Gentiles some of the Jews acted out in violence because they were jealous. Verse 13:45

6. How is Exodus 12:41 in the Old Testament like Acts of the Apostles 13:20 in the New Testament?

    The Old Testament speaks of four hundred and thirty years. The New Testament speaks of four hundred and fifty years.

Acts of the Apostles 14

QUESTIONS AND RESPONSES

1. What happened at Iconium at the Jewish synagogue when Paul and Barnabas were there?

    When Paul and Barnabas were at the Jewish synagogue at Iconium, they spoke out boldly of the Lord and the Jews and Gentiles attempted to kill them but they fled to the cities of Lystra and Derbe. Verse 14:6

2. Who told the crowds to turn from worshipping idols to the living God who made heaven and earth and sea and all that is in them?

    Barnabas and Paul told the crowds to turn from worshipping idols to worshipping the living God of heaven, earth and sea. Verse 14:15

3. Who healed the crippled man at Lystra?

    Paul healed the crippled man of Lystra. Verses 14:8-10

4. Paul and Barnabas continued to proclaim the good news. They told their disciples to _____ in _____.

    Paul and Barnabas told their disciples to persevere in faith. verse 14:22

5. How did they appoint the presbyters in each church?

    They appointed the presbyters in each church with prayer and fasting. Verse 14:23

6. How is Psalm 146:6 in the Old Testament like Acts of the Apostles 14:15b in the New Testament?

    Both verses are about who made heaven and earth.

Acts of the Apostles 15

QUESTIONS AND RESPONSE

1. What was the journey of Paul and Barnabas through Phoenicia and Samaria to tell all the brothers about? What was the great news of great joy?

    The journey of Paul and Barnabas through Phoenicia and Samaria was about the conversion of the Gentiles because of the signs and wonders God had worked. Verses 15:2, 15:3 and 15:12

2. What are some of the dietary laws stated by James?

    Some of the dietary laws stated by James were to avoid pollution of idols, unlawful marriages and the meat and blood of strangled animals. verse 15:20

3. What was the message in the letter of the apostles delivered by Judas and Silas?

    The message in the letter of the apostles delivered by Judas and Silas was that it is the decision of the Holy Spirit and us not to place on you any burden beyond these necessities, namely, to abstain from meat sacrificed to idols, from blood, from meat of strangled animals and from unlawful marriage. Verses 15:28 and 15:29

4. What were Paul and Barnabas doing as they remained in Antioch?

    Paul and Barnabas remained in Antioch to continue teaching and proclaiming the Word of God. Verses 15:30 and 15:35

5. When Paul and Barnabas separated, who did they each take with them?

    Paul took Silas with him to Syria and Cilicia. Barnabas took Mark with him to Cypus. Verses 15:38-15:41

6. How is Leviticus 3:17 in the Old Testament like Acts 15:20 in the New Testament?

    Both verses are about not to partake in any fat (meat) or blood.

Acts of the Apostles 16

QUESTIONS AND RESPONSES

1. Who had a Jewish mother that was a believer and a Greek father?

   Timothy was a believer who had a Jewish mother and a Greek father. Verse 16:1

2. Where were Paul and Silas not to preach?

   Paul and Silas were prevented by the Holy Spirit to preach in Asia. Verse 16:6

3. In his vision, Paul was to go where to preach?

   In his vision, Paul was to go to Macedonia to preach. Verse 16:9

4. Who became a believer and paid attention to what Paul was saying? What did she do in response?

   Lydia paid attention to what Paul was saying and became a believer. She was a dealer of purple cloth. Her whole household was baptized and then she offered them a place to stay. Verses 16:14 and 16:15

5. What happened about midnight when Paul and Silas were praying and singing hymns to God and the prisoners were listening?

   When Paul and Silas were praying and singing at about midnight, there was a severe earthquake that the foundations of the jail shook; all the doors flew open, and the chains of all were pulled loose. Verse 16:26

6. How is Acts of the Apostles 16:37 like Acts of the Apostles 22:25 in the New Testament?

   Both verses are about a Roman citizen being beaten without having been tried,

Acts of the Apostles 17:32

QUESTIONS AND RESPONSES

1. What did the Jews do when they became jealous of Paul and Silas who were discussing the scriptures in Thessalonica?

    When the Jews became jealous of Paul and Silas, they recruited some worthless men loitering in the public square, formed a mob, and set the city in turmoil. Verse 17:5

2. Where did Paul and Silas go during the night? What did they do at this place?

    During the night Paul and Silas went to the synagogue of the Jews and preached and taught the scriptures. Verses 17:10 and 17:11

3. Paul was sent ahead to Athens. What did he find happening there?

    When Paul went to Athens, he found the city full of idols. Verse 17:16

4. Paul then went to Areopagus. What did he find happening there?

    When Paul went to Areopagus, he found the worship of images of gold, silver and stone. Verse 17:29

5. Why are we not to think of God as an image fashioned from gold or silver or stone by the human art of imagination?

    We are not to think of God as an image of gold or silver or stone because of the day He will come to judge us and because of the resurrection and our hope for eternal life. Verses 17:30 and 17:31

6. How is Genesis 1:1 in the Old Testament like Acts of the Apostles 17:24 in the New Testament?

    Both verses are about the creation of heaven and earth.

Acts of the Apostles 18

QUESTIONS AND RESPONSE

1. What did the Lord say to Paul one night in a vision when he was in Corinth?

    One night in a vision the Lord said to Paul: "Do not be afraid. Go on speaking, and do not be silent, for I am with you. No one will attack and harm you, for I have many people in this city." Verse 18:9

2. What did the Jews in Achaia do to Paul and what did they say about him?

    The Jews in Achaia rose against Paul and brought him to the tribunal saying that Paul was inducing people to worship God contrary to the law. Verses 18:12 and 18:13

3. Where did Paul sail to next and who went along, too?

    Paul sailed to Syria and Priscilla and Aquila went with him. Verse 18:18

4. Where did Paul go next and what did he do there?

    Next Paul went to Ephesus to the synagogues and held discussions with the Jews. Verse 18:19

5. Who was Apollos, the Jew, and what did he do?

    Apollos was a Jew, an eloquent speaker and an authority on the scriptures. Verse 18:24

6. How is Numbers 6:18 in the Old Testament like Acts of the Apostles 18:18 in the New Testament?

    Both verses are about cutting or shaving of the hair to represent one who is dedicated and vowing to be sacred.

Acts of the Apostles 19

QUESTIONS AND RESPONSES

1. What happened when Paul was in Ephesus when he first arrived?

    When Paul first arrived in Ephesus, he laid his hands on the disciples and the Holy Spirit came upon them and they spoke in tongues and prophesied. Verse 19:6

2. What happened as a result of the mighty deeds God accomplished at the hands of Paul?

    As a result of the mighty deeds God accomplished, many Jews and Greeks had diseases that left them and evil spirits came out of them. Verses 19:11 and 19:12

3. What practices did some of the Jews and Greeks in Ephesus have before they came believers?

    Some of the Jews and Greeks practiced magic before they became believers. Verse 19:19

4. Who were the two people assisting Paul that he sent to Macedonia?

    Two people who assisted Paul, Timothy and Erastus, were sent to Macedonia. verse 19:22

5. Who was known as the great goddess of Asia? Do we believe in this goddess? Why?

    A great goddess of Asia was Artemis. We do not believe in this goddess because the people were worshipping silver stones that looked like her. Verses 19:24 and 19:27

6. How is Acts of the Apostles 8:16 in the New Testament like Acts of the Apostles 19:5 in the New Testament?

    Both verses are about being baptized in the Lord Jesus.

Acts of the Apostles 20

QUESTIONS AND RESPONSES

1. How long did Paul stay in Greece? Why did he leave?

    Paul stayed three months in Greece and he left because a plot was made against bim by the Jews. Verses 20:2 and 20:3

2. Why did Paul restore Eutychus to life?

    Paul restored Eutychus to life so it could be related to the resurrection. Note from Verse 20:7

3. Where was Paul in a hurry to go and for what day?

    Paul was in a hurry to go to Jerusalem for the day of Pentecost. verse 20:16

4. What was the great desire of Paul to finish?

    The great desire of Paul was to finish his ministry that he received from the Lord Jesus, to bear witness to the gospel of God's grace. Verse 20:24

5. What did Paul do when he finished speaking?

    When Paul finished speaking, he knelt down and prayed with them all. Verse 20:36

6. How is 1 Kings 17:21 in the Old Testament like Acts of Apostles 20:10 in the New Testament?

    Both verses are about life within or life restored.

Acts of the Apostles 21

QUESTIONS AND RESPONSE

1. When Paul left Tyre, what did everyone do including the women and children?

   When Paul left Tyre, everyone knelt on the beach to pray. Verse 21:5

2. Where did Paul go when he arrived at Caesarea?

   When Paul arrived at Caesarea, he went to the house of Philip, the evangelist, who was one of the seven and stayed with him. Verse 21:8

3. Where did Paul go when he arrived in Jerusalem?

   When Paul arrived in Jerusalem, he went to the house of Mnason, a disciple of long standing, and stayed with him. Verse 21:16

4. What did the Jews from Asia do to Paul?

   The Jews from Asia stirred up the crowd in the temple, laid hands on him, seized him, dragged him out of the temple and then he was arrested. Verses 21:27-21:30

5. After Paul received permission to speak to the people, what language did he speak to them in?

   After Paul received permission to speak to the people, he spoke to them in Hebrew. Verse 21:40

6. How is Numbers 6:5 in the Old Testament like Acts of the Apostles 21:23 in the New Testament?

   Both verses are about a vow.

Acts of the Apostles 22

QUESTIONS AND RESPONSES

1. What were some of the things Paul told the Jews in Jerusalem about himself?

    Paul told the Jews that he was a Jew born in Tarsus and was educated strictly in our ancestral law and was zealous for God. Verse 22:3

2. Where was Paul led after he was blinded by the light of Jesus?

    Paul was led into Damascus. Verse 22:11

3. After Ananias told Paul to regain his sight, what did Paul tell the Jews to do?

    Paul asked the Jews to be a witness, to be baptized and have sins washed away. Verse 22:16

4. What kept Paul from being whipped and put in prison?

    Paul did not get whipped and put in prison because he was born a Roman citizen. Verse 22:26 and 22:28.

5. Who freed Paul?

    The commander freed Paul. verse 22:29

6. How is Luke 24:48 in the New Testament like Acts of the Apostles 22:15 in the New Testament?

    Both verses are about being witnesses of Christ.

Acts of the Apostles 23

QUESTIONS AND RESPONSES

1. What was the topic of what the Pharisees and Sadducees were disputing?

    The Pharisees and Sadducees were disputing the topic of the resurrection. Verse 23:6

2. What was the plot that the Jews made concerning Paul?

    The Jews made a plot not to eat or drink until they killed Paul. Verse 23:12

3. What information about Paul was secretly given to the commander?

    The information that was secretly given to the commanders about Paul was that the Jews were planning to kill bim. Verses 23:19-23:21

4. What were the soldiers commanded to do?

    The soldiers were commanded to escort Paul by night to Antipatris. Verse 23:31

5. What did the letter to the governor contain that was important information about Paul?

    The letter emphasized that Paul was a Roman citizen and that there was a lack of evidence that Paul was guilty of a crime. Notes of Verses 23:26-23:30

6. How is exodus 22:27b in the Old Testament like Acts of the Apostles 23:5b in the New Testament?

    Both verses are about not cursing the ruler of your people.

Acts of the Apostles 24

QUESTIONS AND RESPONSE

1. Who were the Nazoreans?

    The Nazoreans were followers of Jesus at Nazareth. Verse 24:5

2. What did Paul tell the governor in his defense?

    Paul told the governor: "I worship the God of our ancestors and I believe everything that is in accordance with the law and written in the prophets. Verse 24:14

3. What did Paul say that he was on trial for?

    Paul said that he was on trial for the resurrection of the dead. Verse 24:21

4. Who left Paul in prison?

    Felix left Paul in prison. verse 24:27

5. Who succeeded Felix in Caesarea?

    Porcius Festus succeeded Felix in Caesarea. verse 24:27

6. How is Luke 23:2 in the New Testament like Acts of the Apostles 24:5 in the New Testament?

    Both verses have these words: "we found this man to be." The verse in Luke ends with "misleading" and the verse in the Acts of the Apostles ends with "a pest".

Acts of the Apostles 25

QUESTIONS AND RESPONSES

1. Where did the chief priests and Jewish leaders present Festus their formal charges against Paul?

    The chief priests and Jewish leaders presented Festus their formal charges against Paul in Jerusalem. Verse 25:1 and 25:2

2. What did Paul say in defense of himself?

    In defense of himself, Paul said: "I have committed no crime either against the Jewish law or against the temple or against Caesar. Verse 25:8

3. Paul appealed to whom?

    Paul appealed to Caesar. verse 25:12

4. What did Festus tell King Agrippa and others present about Paul?

    Festus told King Agrippa and others present that he found Paul to have done nothing deserving of death. Verse 25:25

5. What seemed senseless to Festus?

    It seemed senseless to Festus to send up a prisoner without indicating the charges against him. Verse 25:27

6. How is Romans 15:25 like the Acts of the Apostles 25:3?

    Romans says: "going" to Jerusalem. Acts of the Apostles says: "sent" to Jerusalem.

Acts of the Apostles 26

QUESTIONS AND RESPONSES

1. What did Paul have to say to King Agrippa?

   Paul said to King Agrippa that he counted himself fortunate to be able to defend himself. Verse 26:2

2. What happened as Paul was traveling on the road to Damascus?

   As Paul was traveling on the road to Damascus he saw a light shine from the sky along with all his traveling companions and he fell to the ground and heard a voice saying to Paul: "Saul, Saul, why are you persecuting me?" Verses 26:13 and 26:14

3. What did the Lord say he appointed Paul to do?

   The Lord said that he appointed Paul to be a servant and a witness, to deliver the Gentiles from the power of Satan and obtain forgiveness of their sins. Verses 26:16-26;18

4. Festus told Paul that he was mad and what was Paul's response?

   When Festus told Paul that he was mad, Paul responded that he was not mad, but he was speaking words of truth and reason, verse 26:25

5. What did the king, governor, Bernice and others say to one another about Paul's response?

   The governor and others were saying that this man, Paul, does not deserve death or imprisonment. Verse 26:31

6. How is Ezekiel 2:1 in the Old Testament like Acts of the Apostles 26:16 in the New Testament?

   Both verses are about stand up or stand on your feet.

Acts of the Apostles 27

QUESTIONS AND RESPONSE

1. Where did Paul and some other prisoners decide to sail to?

    Paul and some other prisoners decided to sail to Italy. Verse 27:1

2. What were some of the difficulties as they sailed to Rome?

    Some of the difficulties as they sailed to Rome were the wind and storms. Verse 27:7

3. What warning did Paul give to them?

    Paul told them the voyage would cause severe damage and heavy loss in cargo and loss of lives, too. Verse 27:10

4. They had all been fasting, but what was Paul's advice for them to do?

    Even though they had been fasting, Paul's advice to them was to take some food. Verse 27:33

5. How many were on ship and bow did they get to safety?

    There were 276 people on the ship. They all got to safety by first throwing out the wheat to make it lighter and those who could swim, swam to shore and those who couldn't swim used planks or debris to get to shore. Verses 27:37-27:44

6. How is Leviticus 16:30 in the Old Testament like Acts of the Apostles 27:9 in the New Testament?

    Both Verses are about the day to fast and be cleansed, a Day of Atonement.

Acts of the Apostles 28

QUESTIONS AND RESPONSES

1. Where did Paul and his companions finally reach?

    Paul and his companions reached the island of Malta. Verse 28:1

2. What did Paul do for the sick people on this island?

    For the sick people on this island, Paul cured them after laying hands on them and prayed with them. Verse 28:8

3. After winter they set sail again and where was it that they arrived and Paul thanked God and took courage?

    After winter, they set sail again and arrived in Rome. Paul then thanked God and took courage. verses 28:14 and 28:15

4. What did Paul say in his testimony to the Jews in Rome?

    In testimony to the Jews in Rome, Paul told them that he had done nothing, but was turned over to the Romans and then released. The Jews objected and obliged him to appeal to Caesar which he did. Verses 28:17-28:19

5. What did Paul do in the two full years he stayed in Rome?

    In the two full years Paul stayed in Rome, he proclaimed the kingdom of God and taught about the Lord Jesus Christ. Verses 28:30-28:31

6. How is Isaiah 6:10 in the Old Testament like Acts of the Apostles 28:27 in the New Testament?

    Both verses are quite the same about people who have ears and do not hear and have eyes that are closed.

FOCUS ON THE "WORD" WITH HOMEMADE BIBLE GAMES

Bible Games are to help us be excited about "the Word of God"!

God inspired the human authors of the Bible. When studying the Bible, it is a good idea to go back to the time and place and contemplate (think about) what the author intended to express.

BIBLE

The word Bible comes from the Greek word - "biblia". The meaning is "books". The Bible has been the best seller for years. It is inspired by God to teach the truths needed for salvation. It is a way for us to better live and communicate with God. It helps us to believe, to love and grow on our journey with the Lord.

The prizes for these games are to be the creativity of the leaders. Children can make some pretty awesome prizes (holy cards, Bible games, pictures, candy, cookies, money, etc.) that teach the young and the old. Prizes of all kinds teach generosity, as well as practicing the skills of giving and receiving. The Bible Studies have such a great potential of teaching and uniting the domestic church, the family. We are all children of God called to be disciples and saints.

SUPER SEVEN
BIBLE GAMES

1. Bible Bingo
2. Bible Memory Card Game
3. Bible Verse Ball Game
4. Bible Verse Ladder Game
5. Books of the Bible Relay Game
6. Can You Get Seven
7. Seven Capital Sins
8. Seven Days of Creation
9. Seven Sacraments
10. Seven Unities of the church

BIBLE BINGO

This game is played like regular Bingo.
The names of the Books of the Bible are what we are looking for.

The top three rows are books from the Old Testament.
There are forty-six books.

The bottom two rows are books from the New Testament.
There are twenty-seven

The Bible cards may be copied, put on poster board and laminated for several times to use.

B I B L E

Genesis	Exodus	Leviticus	Numbers	Deuteronomy
Joshua	Judges	Ruth	1 Samuel	2 Samuel
1 Kings	2 Kings	Jesus	1 Chronicles	2 Chronicles
Matthew	Mark	Luke	John	Acts of the Apostles
Romans	1 Corinthians	2 Corinthians	Galatians	Ephesians
B	I	B	L	E

B I B L E

2 Kings	Exodus	Leviticus	Numbers	Deuteronomy
Joshua	Judges	Ruth	1 Samuel	2 Samuel
1 Kings	Ezra	Jesus	1 Chronicles	2 Chronicles
Ephesians	Mark	Luke	John	Acts of the Apostles
Romans	1 Corinthians	2 Corinthians	Galatians	Philippians
B	I	B	L	E

B I B L E

Genesis	Nehemiah	Leviticus	Numbers	Deuteronomy
Joshua	Judges	Ruth	1 Samuel	2 Samuel
1 Kings	2 Kings	Jesus	1 Chronicles	2 Chronicles
Matthew	Mark	Luke	John	Acts of the Apostles
Romans	1 Corinthians	2 Corinthians	Galatians	Colossians
B	I	B	L	E

B I B L E

Genesis	Exodus	Tobit	Judith	Deuteronomy
Joshua	Judges	Ruth	1 Samuel	2 Samuel
1 Kings	2 Kings	Jesus	1 Chronicles	2 Chronicles
Matthew	1 Thessalonians	Luke	John	Acts of the Apostles
Romans	1 Corinthians	2 Corinthians	2 Thessalonians	Ephesians
B	I	B	L	E

B I B L E

Genesis	Exodus	Leviticus	Judith	Esther
Joshua	Judges	Ruth	1 Samuel	2 Samuel
1 Kings	2 Kings	Jesus	1 Chronicles	2 Chronicles
Matthew	Mark	Luke	John	1 Timothy
Romans	2 Timothy	2 Corinthians	Galatians	Ephesians

B I B L E

B I B L E

Genesis	Exodus	Leviticus	Numbers	Deuteronomy
Joshua	1 Maccabees	Ruth	1 Samuel	2 Samuel
1 Kings	2 Kings	Jesus	1 Chronicles	2 Maccabees
Philemon	Mark	Luke	John	Acts of the Apostles
Romans	1 Corinthians	2 Corinthians	Titus	Ephesians
B	I	B	L	E

B I B L E

Job	Exodus	Leviticus	Numbers	Deuteronomy
Psalms	Judges	Ruth	1 Samuel	2 Samuel
1 Kings	2 Kings	Jesus	1 Chronicles	2 Chronicles
Hebrews	Mark	Luke	James	Acts of the Apostles
Romans	1 Corinthians	2 Corinthians	Galatians	Ephesians
B	I	B	L	E

B I B L E

Genesis	Exodus	Leviticus	Numbers	Deuteronomy
Joshua	Judges	Ruth	Ecclesiastes	2 Samuel
Proverbs	2 Kings	Jesus	1 Chronicles	2 Chronicles
Matthew	2 Peter	Luke	John	Acts of the Apostles
Romans	1 Corinthians	2 Corinthians	1 Peter	Ephesians
B	**I**	**B**	**L**	**E**

B I B L E

Genesis	Song of Songs	Leviticus	Numbers	Deuteronomy
Joshua	Judges	Wisdom	1 Samuel	2 Samuel
1 Kings	2 Kings	Jesus	1 Chronicles	Sirach
3 John	Mark	Luke	John	Acts of the Apostles
Romans	1 Corinthians	2 Corinthians	2 John	Ephesians
B	**I**	**B**	**L**	**E**

B I B L E

Isaiah	Song of Songs	Leviticus	Numbers	Jeremiah
Joshua	Judges	Wisdom	1 Samuel	2 Samuel
Lamentations	2 Kings	Jesus	1 Chronicles	Sirach
3 John	Mark	Jude	John	Acts of the Apostles
Romans	1 John	2 Corinthians	2 John	Ephesians

B I B L E

B I B L E

Baruch	Song of Songs	Leviticus	Numbers	Deuteronomy
Joshua	Judges	Wisdom	Ezekiel	2 Samuel
1 Kings	2 Kings	Jesus	Daniel	Sirach
3 John	Revelation	Luke	John	Acts of the Apostles
Romans	1 Corinthians	2 Corinthians	2 John	Matthew
B	I	B	L	E

Genesis	Song of Songs	Leviticus	Numbers	Hosea
Joshua	Judges	Wisdom	1 Samuel	Joel
1 Kings	2 Kings	Jesus	Amos	Sirach
3 John	Galatians	Luke	John	Acts of the Apostles
Romans	Matthew	2 Corinthians	2 John	Ephesians
B	I	B	L	E

B	I	B	L	E
Obadiah	Song of Songs	Leviticus	Numbers	Deuteronomy
Joshua	Jonah	Wisdom	Micah	Nahum
Habakkuk	2 Kings	Jesus	1 Chronicles	Sirach
3 John	Mark	Hebrews	John	Acts of the Apostles
Romans	1 Corinthians	Galatians	2 John	Ephesians
B	I	B	L	E

B I B L E

Obadiah	Song of Songs	Zechariah	Haggai	Zephaniah
Joshua	Jonah	Wisdom	Micah	Nahum
Habakkuk	2 Kings	Jesus	1 Chronicles	Sirach
3 John	Mark	Hebrews	Jude	Revelation
Romans	1 Corinthians	Galatians	2 John	Ephesians
B	**I**	**B**	**L**	**E**

B I B L E

Ruth	Malachi	Leviticus	Numbers	Deuteronomy
Judges	Jonah	Wisdom	Micah	Nahum
Habakkuk	2 Kings	Jesus	1 Chronicles	Sirach
Luke	Mark	Matthew	John	Acts of the Apostles
Romans	1 Corinthians	Galatians	2 John	Ephesians
B	**I**	**B**	**L**	**E**

Obadiah	Song of Songs	Leviticus	Numbers	Deuteronomy
Joshua	Exodus	Genesis	2 Maccabees	Nahum
Habakkuk	2 Kings	Jesus	1 Chronicles	Sirach
3 John	Mark	Hebrews	John	Acts of the Apostles
Romans	Luke	1 Corinthians	2 John	Ephesians
B	I	B	L	E

B I B L E

B	I	B	L	E
Obadiah	Song of Songs	Leviticus	Numbers	Deuteronomy
Joshua	Jonah	Wisdom	Micah	1 Maccabees
Esther	Judith	Jesus	1 Chronicles	Sirach
3 John	Mark	Hebrews	John	Acts of the Apostles
Romans	1 Corinthians	Galatians	2 John	1 John
B	I	B	L	E

B I B L E

Ezra	Song of Songs	Leviticus	Numbers	Deuteronomy
Joshua	Jonah	Wisdom	Micah	Nahum
Habakkuk	2 Kings	Jesus	Tobit	Nehemiah
2 Peter	James	Hebrews	John	Acts of the Apostles
Romans	1 Corinthians	Galatians	2 John	Ephesians
B	I	B	L	E

B I B L E

B	I	B	L	E
Obadiah	2 Chronicles	1 Kings	2 Samuel	Deuteronomy
Joshua	Jonah	Wisdom	Micah	Nahum
Habakkuk	2 Kings	Jesus	1 Chronicles	Sirach
3 John	Mark	Hebrews	Philemon	Titus
Romans	1 Corinthians	Galatians	2 John	Ephesians

B I B L E

B I B L E

Obadiah	Song of Songs	Leviticus	Numbers	Deuteronomy
Joshua	Job	Psalms	Proverbs	Nahum
Habakkuk	2 Kings	Jesus	1 Chronicles	Sirach
3 John	Mark	Hebrews	John	2 Timothy
Romans	1 Corinthians	Galatians	Colossians	Ephesians
B	**I**	**B**	**L**	**E**

B I B L E

B	I	B	L	E
Obadiah	Song of Songs	Leviticus	Numbers	Deuteronomy
Joshua	Jonah	Wisdom	Micah	Nahum
Habakkuk	Baruch	Jesus	Daniel	Amos
3 John	Titus	Hebrews	John	Acts of the Apostles
Romans	1 Corinthians	Galatians	Jude	Ephesians
B	I	B	L	E

"TEN COMMANDMENT BIBLE MEMORY GAME"

"TEN COMMANDMENTS"
Exodus 20:1-17
Deuteronomy 5:7-21
OLD TESTAMENT
All cards are to be passed out.
Each player takes a turn to match two cards.
The player with most matches at the end of
the game wins.

Home made cards are to be made with four sets of the Ten Commandments. The cards will last longer, if they are laminated or covered with the laminate available in the household section in the store by the shelf lining paper.

THE TEN COMMANDMENTS

1. I am the Lord your God, you shall not have strange gods before me.

2. You shall not use the name of the Lord your God in vain.

3. Remember to keep holy the Lord's day.

4. Honor your father and your mother.

5. You shall not kill.

6. You shall not commit adultery.

7. You shall not steal.

8. You shall not lie or bear false witness against your neighbor.

9. You shall not covet your neighbor's wife.

10. You shall not covet your neighbor's goods.

BIBLE VERSE BALL GAME

This is a game of memorization.
Why do we memorize Bible verses?
To help us take God's Word to heart.
To help us live God's Word by our actions.
To guide us on the right path.

Repetition is the key to memorization.

It is best to have seven in a circle.

The leader says the name of the book and then the chapter and then the verse. Then everyone is to say it together for at least three times. The leader will then begin by saying the name of the book and tossing the ball to someone and they are to say the number of the chapter. They toss it to someone who then says the number of the verse. Then they toss the ball and that person says the first word of the verse. That person tosses the ball and then that person says the second word of the verse, etc. until the verse has been said.

If someone needs help, all are to say the Word.

ENJOY SHARING GOD'S WORD!!!

It works good to have laminated copies of the verses for the leaders. The verses laminated to recipe cards works good.

Matthew 6:21

"For where your treasure is, there also your heart is."

Matthew 7:12

"Do to others whatever you would have them do to you. This is the law and the prophets."

Mark 1:17

Jesus said to them, "Come after me, and I will make you fishers of men."

Mark 3:35

"For whoever does the will of God is my brother and sister and mother."

Luke 4:8

"You shall worship the Lord, your God, and Him alone shall you serve."

Luke 6:12

"In those days He departed to the mountain to pray, and He spent the night in prayer to God,"

John 6:27

"Do not work for food that perishes but for the food that endures for eternal life, which the Son of Man will give you."

John 7:24

"Stop judging by appearances, but judge justly."

Acts of the Apostles 4:31

"As they prayed, the place where they were gathered shook, and they were all filled with the Holy Spirit and continued the word of God with boldness."

Acts of the Apostles 5:42

"And all day long, both at the temple and in their homes, they did not stop teaching and proclaiming the Messiah, Jesus."

BIBLE VERSE
LADDER GAME

This game consists of seven verses of the
first seven chaptersof a book from the Bible.

The Bible Verse Titles are in bigger print on the bigger craft stick.

Each word of the Bible verse on a craft stick
is to gounder the title to make a ladder.

People are divided into teams. The first team to have
their seven ladders in order is the winner!

BIBLE

To make these sets for the Ladder Game with the Bible verses just use the craft
sticks (Jumbo and Regular) that can be bought at Hobby Lobby or Wal-Mart.
Red and black sharpie markers work good too.

BIBLE

Matthew 1:1
"The book of the genealogy of Jesus Christ, the son of David, the son of Abraham."

Matthew 2:23
He went and dwelt in a town called Nazareth, so that what had been spoken through the prophets might be fulfilled, "He shall be called a Nazorean."

Matthew 3:11
"I am baptizing you with water, for repentance, but the one who is coming after me is mightier than I."

Matthew 4:19
He said to them, "Come after me, and I will make you fishers of men."

Matthew 5:16
"Just so, your light must shine before others, that they may see your good deeds and glorify your heavenly Father."

Matthew 6:21
"For where your treasure is, there also your heart is."

Matthew 7:12
"Do to others whatever you would have them do to you. This is the law and the prophets."

BIBLE VERSE LADDER GAME
MARK

BIBLE

Mark 1:17
Jesus said to them, "Come after me, and I will make you fishers of men."

Mark 2:17
Jesus heard this and said to them, "Those who are well do not need a physician, but the sick do. I did not come to call the righteous but sinners."

Mark 3:35
"For whoever does the will of God is my brother and sister and mother."

Mark 4:41
They were filled with great awe and said to one another, "Who then is this whom even the wind and sea obey?"

Mark 5:19
"Go home to your family and announce to them all that the Lord in his pity has done for you."

Mark 6:11
"Whatever place does not welcome you or listen to you, leave there and shake the dust off your feet in testimony against them."

Mark 7:8
"You disregard God's commandment but cling to human tradition."

BIBLE

Luke 1:45
"Blessed are you who believed that what was spoken to you by the Lord would be fulfilled."

Luke 2:14
"Glory to God in the highest and on earth peace to those on whom His favor rests."

Luke 3:11
"Whoever has two cloaks should share with the person who has none. And whoever has food should do likewise."

Luke 4:8
"You shall worship the Lord, your God, and Him alone shall you serve."

Luke 5:32
"I have not come to call the righteous to repentance but sinners."

Luke 6:12
"In those days He departed to the mountain to pray, and He spent the night in prayer to God."

Luke 7:50b
"Your faith has saved you; go in peace."

BIBLE VERSE LADDER GAME
JOHN

BIBLE

John 1:1
"In the beginning was the Word, and the Word was with God, and the Word was God."

John 2:23
"While he was in Jerusalem for the feast of the Passover, many began to believe in his name when they saw the signs he was doing."

John 3:16
"For God so loved the world that he gave his only Son, so that everyone who believes in him might not perish but might have eternal life."

John 4:34
Jesus said to them, "My food is to do the will of the one who sent me and to finish his work."

John 5:47
"But if you do not believe his writings how will you believe my words?"

John 6:27
"Do not work for food that perishes but for the food that endures for eternal life, which the Son of Man will give you."

John 7:24
"Stop judging by appearances, but judge justly."

BIBLE

Acts of the Apostles 1:14a
"All these devoted themselves with one accord in prayer."

Acts of the Apostles 2:42
"They devoted themselves to the teaching of the apostles and to the communal life, to the breaking of the bread and to the prayers."

Acts of the Apostles 3::23
"Everyone who does not listen to that prophet will be cut off from the people."

Acts of the Apostles 4:31
"As they prayed, the place where they were gathered shook, and they were all filled with the Holy Spirit and continued the word of God with boldness."

Acts of the Apostles 5:42
"And all day long, both at the temple and in their homes, they did not stop teaching and proclaiming the Messiah, Jesus."

Acts of the Apostles 6:2b
"It is not right for us to neglect the word of God to serve at table."

Acts of the Apostles 7:55
"But he, filled with the Holy Spirit, looked up intently to heaven and saw the glory of God and Jesus standing at the right hand of God."

BOOKS OF THE BIBLE
RELAY GAME

Teams are selected

It is preferred to have approximately seven people on each team.

The names of the Books of the Bible are on half copy paper
sheets attached to poster board and laminated.

Each set is put in a box on the other side of the large room or gym.
Relay lines are formed for each team.

At the set starting time, each person on a team runs
to get the name of the book in the Bible.

The team puts them in order.

The first team who correctly completes the Books
being put in order is the winner.

One to three games are usually played at each session.

To make two sets of cards for the relay game: copy two sets of the following
pages that have the names of the books of the Bible on, cut each page in half
and put on poster board. Copy fourteen pages for the other side with the
words: "New Testament" and then laminate for longer lasting cards. (White
out the page number, if you would like to before copying.)

Matthew

Mark

Luke

John

Acts of the
Apostles

Romans

1 Corinthians

2 Corinthians

Galatians

Ephesians

Philippians

Colossians

1 Thessalonians

2 Thessalonians

1 Timothy

2 Timothy

Titus

Philemon

Hebrews

James

1 Peter

2 Peter

1 John

2 John

3 John

Jude

Revelation

New Testament

New Testament

CAN YOU GET SEVEN?

7

The goal of the game is for the disciple to get seven points by answering the questions correctly or by being saved by two followers

The disciple receives two points for each correct answer.

The disciple may be saved by a follower answering correctly and would get one point.

At any time the disciple and the followers have the incorrect answers, they have to quit and a new disciple and two followers are chosen.

If the disciple gets seven points, they are all winners.

New copies of the questions for the participants works good.

CAN YOU GET SEVEN? QUESTIONS.

1. The Bible is a collection of:

    a. letters
    b. books
    c. novels

2. The Bible is often called:

    a. Testament
    b. scripture
    c. covenant

3. The Bible has how many books:

    a. seventy
    b. forty-nine
    c. seventy-three

4. The Bible was written by different authors with different:

    a. letters
    b. psalms
    c. styles

5. The Bible was composed in the different languages, name one of them:

    a. Jewish
    b. Italian
    c. Hebrew

6. The word "testament" means:

    a. covenant
    b. examine

c. miracle

7. The Old Testament is about:

   a. The Holy Spirit and the Greeks
   b. God and Jewish people
   c. the apostles

8. The New Testament is about:

   a. Jesus and Christian people
   b. Jewish ancestors and Mary
   c. Adam and Eve

9. The Old Testament has how many books?

   a. fifty-one
   b. forty-six
   c. sixty-three

10. The New Testament has how many books?

   a. twenty-one
   b. thirty-four
   c. twenty-seven

11. The Bible is:

   a. a testament
   b. the living Word of God
   c. the story of Noah and the Ark

12. The Old Testament in the Bible was written:

   a. in the nine centuries before Jesus' birth
   b. two thousand years before Jesus' birth

c. in the fifteenth century before Jesus

13. The New Testament in the Bible was written:

    a. in the century before Jesus' birth
    b. in the century after Jesus' birth
    c. in the year Jesus died

14. The Old Testament has four main collections of books called:

    a. the prophetic books, the historical books, the gospels, the wisdom books
    b. the Pentateuch, the wisdom books, the prophetic books, the historical books
    c. the letters, the prophetic books, the wisdom books, the historical books

15. The Bible is always read in:

    a. school
    b. library
    c. church

16. The Gospel that is primarily about signs is:

    a. Mark
    b. John
    c. Luke

17. The New Testament has three main collections of books called:

    a. the New Testament letters, the wisdom books, the catholic letters
    b. the gospels, the prophetic books, the wisdom books
    c. the catholic letters, the New Testament letters, the gospels

18. The Gospels in the New Testament are:

    a. Matthew, Mark, Luke, John
    b. Peter, Paul, Matthew, Acts, John
    c. Matthew, Luke, Peter, Andrew, Timothy

19. The Bible is the speech of:

    a. Mary
    b. Moses
    c. God

20. The Bible was written under the breath of:

    a. Joseph
    b. the Holy Spirit
    c. the apostles

21. Why we read the Bible is written in 2 Timothy 3:16, so why do we?

    a. for teaching, correcting, training, improving
    b. for judging, teaching, improving, selecting
    c. for speaking, judging, writing, training

22. The Protestant Old Testament Bible has how many books?

    a. forty-six
    b. thirty-nine
    c. forty-seven

23. The Catholic Bible has how many more books than the Protestants?

    a. nine
    b. three
    c. seven

24. The teaching about Purgatory and praying for the dead is in which book of the Catholic Bible?

    a. Matthew
    b. Luke
    c. 2 Maccabees

25. The first pope and the beginning of the Catholic Church is in the:

    a. the book of Genesis
    b. the New Testament
    c. the Old Testament

26. The Bible can be described as:

    a. a fable in ancient times
    b. a blueprint in-living before leaving earth
    c. a fiction book

27. At what part of the Mass are Bible readings read?

    a. Liturgy of the Word
    b. the Preparation of Gifts
    c. Liturgy of the Eucharist

28. They synoptic Gospels are:

    a. Mark, Luke, John
    b. Matthew, Luke, Mark
    c. John, Matthew, Luke

29. What is a good way to use the Bible?

    a. for decoration
    b. for a prayer book
    c. for making money

30. What Book of the Bible has a chapter with Jesus praying to God?

   a. Matthew 21
   b. Acts of the Apostles 10
   c. John 17

31. Where is the "Our Father" in the Bible?

   a. Genesis 7
   b. Matthew 6
   c. John 17

32. Where are "The Beatitudes" in the Bible?

   a. Luke 10
   b. Psalm 68
   c. Matthew 5

CAN YOU GET SEVEN? ANSWERS

1. The Bible is a collection of:

    a. letters
    b. books
    c. novels

2. The Bible is often called:

    a. Testament
    b. scripture
    c. covenant

3. The Bible has how many books:

    a. seventy
    b. forty-nine
    c. seventy-three

4. The Bible was written by different authors with different:

    a. letters
    b. psalms
    c. styles

5. The Bible was composed in the different languages, name one of them:

    a. Jewish
    b. Italian
    c. Hebrew

6. The word "testament" means:

    a. covenant
    b. examine

c. miracle

7. The Old Testament is about:

   a. The Holy Spirit and the Greeks
   b. God and Jewish people
   c. the apostles

8. The New Testament is about:

   a. Jesus and Christian people
   b. Jewish ancestors and Mary
   c. Adam and Eve

9. The Old Testament has how many books?

   a. fifty-one
   b. forty-six
   c. sixty-three

10. The New Testament has how many books?

    a. twenty-one
    b. thirty-four
    c. twenty-seven

11. The Bible is:

    a. a testament
    b. the living Word of God
    c. the story of Noah and the Ark

12. The Old Testament in the Bible was written:

    a. in the nine centuries before Jesus' birth
    b. two thousand years before Jesus' birth

c. in the fifteenth century before Jesus

13. The New Testament in the Bible was written:

    a. in the century before Jesus' birth
    b. in the century after Jesus' birth
    c. in the year Jesus died

14. The Old Testament has four main collections of books called:

    a. the prophetic books, the historical books, the gospels, the wisdom books
    b. the Pentateuch, the wisdom books, the prophetic books, the historical books
    c. the letters, the prophetic books, the wisdom books, the historical books

15. The Bible is always read in:

    a. school
    b. library
    c. church

16. The Gospel that is primarily about signs is:

    a. Mark
    b. John
    c. Luke

17. The New Testament has three main collections of books called:

    a. the New Testament letters, the wisdom books, the catholic letters
    b. the gospels, the prophetic books, the wisdom books
    c. the catholic letters, the New Testament letters, the gospels

18. The Gospels in the New Testament are:

    a. Matthew, Mark, Luke, John
    b. Peter, Paul, Matthew, Acts, John
    c. Matthew, Luke, Peter, Andrew, Timothy

19. The Bible is the speech of:

    a. Mary
    b. Moses
    c. God

20. The Bible was written under the breath of:

    a. Joseph
    b. the Holy Spirit
    c. the apostles

21. Why we read the Bible is written in 2 Timothy 3:16, so why do we?

    a. for teaching, correcting, training, improving
    b. for judging, teaching, improving, selecting
    c. for speaking, judging, writing, training

22. The Protestant Old Testament Bible has how many books?

    a. forty-six
    b. thirty-nine
    c. forty-seven

23. The Catholic Bible has how many more books than the Protestants?

    a. nine
    b. three
    c. seven

24. The teaching about Purgatory and praying for the dead is in which book of the Catholic Bible?

    a. Matthew
    b. Luke
    c. 2 Maccabees

25. The first pope and the beginning of the Catholic Church is in the:

    a. the book of Genesis
    b. the New Testament
    c. the Old Testament

26. The Bible can be described as:

    a. a fable in ancient times
    b. a blueprint in-living before leaving earth
    c. a fiction book

27. At what part of the Mass are Bible readings read?

    a. Liturgy of the Word
    b. the Preparation of Gifts
    c. Liturgy of the Eucharist

28. They synoptic Gospels are:

    a. Mark, Luke, John
    b. Matthew, Luke, Mark
    c. John, Matthew, Luke

29. What is a good way to use the Bible?

    a. for decoration
    b. for a prayer book
    c. for making money

30. What Book of the Bible has a chapter with Jesus praying to God?

    a. Matthew 21
    b. Acts of the Apostles 10
    c. John 17

31. Where is the "Our Father" in the Bible?

    a. Genesis 7
    b. Matthew 6
    c. John 17

32. Where are "The Beatitudes" in the Bible?

    a. Luke 10
    b. Psalm 68
    c. Matthew 5

SUPER SEVEN
WORD GAME

THE SEVEN CAPITAL SINS
Sins do NOT build a church.

pride

covetousness

lust

anger

gluttony

envy

sloth

Each sin is explained by those who are dressed with a black robe or cloth.

The sign with the name of the sin and where it is in in the Bible and how to avoid it is to be presented from the use of the signs that are made.

Then the other participants are invited
to act out how they want to "get rid of sin".

For example: throwing water and/or marshmallows.
(This is to be done outside).

Copies of the signs are to be cut and laminated
so they are ready to be used several times.

Pride

Lust

Anger

Gluttony

Envy

Sloth

Covetousness

Pride is self-love and the opposite of living for God.
Practice humility and self-denial.
Proverbs 16:18

Covetousness is love of worldly goods.
Practice generosity and kindness.
1 Timothy 6:10

Lust is wanting another person's husband or wife.
Practice thankfulness and sacrificing.
Colossians 3:5

Anger is the source from which injuries of
another flow.
Practice calmness and peace.
Matthew 5:22

Envy is ingratitude and belittling another.
Practice prayer and the interests of another.
Acts of the Apostles 7:9

Gluttony is an unregulated love for food or drink.
Practice fasting and self-denial.
1 Corinthians 10:31

Sloth is a laziness of mind and body and spiritual growth.
Practice prayer, the sacraments and spiritual readings.
Exodus 5:8

SEVEN DAYS OF CREATION

The First Day: Light

Genesis 1:3	Exodus 13:21
Job 3:16	Psalms 27:1
Proverbs 16:15	Daniel 2:22
Amos 5:18	

The Second Day; Land and Water and Sky

Leviticus 25:19	Deuteronomy 1:25
Numbers 5:17	Psalms 1:3
Isaiah 55:10	Pslams 89:37
Genesis 1:8	

The Third Day; Grass and Flowers and Trees

Proverbs 19:12	Psalms 90:5
Isaiah 40:8	Song of Songs 2:12
Jeremiah 17:8	Job 14:7
Genesis 1:11	

The Fourth Day: Sun and Moon and Stars

Ecclestiastes 1:9	Psalms 121:6
Joshua 10:13	Psalms 72:7
Judges 5:20	Job 38:7
Genesis 1:16	

The Fifth Day: Fish and Birds

Numbers 11:5	Deuteronomy 4:18
Psalms 8:8	Isaiah 31:5
Jeremiah 5:27	Psalms 104:17
Genesis 1:20	

The Sixth Day: Animals and People

Genesis 7:2	Deuteronomy 14:6
Genesis 8:8-19	Nehemiah 8:5
Isaiah 40:1	Psalms 114:15

Psalms 29:11

The Seventh Day: Rest and Holy

Deuteronomy 5:12	1 Samuel 2:2
Nehemiah 8:9	Exodus 20:8
Job 3:17	Exodus 20:11
Genesis 2:2	

This can be built individually or have two sets for team competition using jenga blocks with the words and verses on the blocks.

SUPER SEVEN
WORD GAME

Seven Sacraments
are for building the church by encountering Jesus.

Baptism .... Galatians 3:27
Confirmation .... John 15:26
Eucharist .... Matthew 26:26-29
(sacraments of initiation)
Matrimony .... Mark 10:6-9
Holy Orders .... 1 Peter 2:5
(sacraments of service)
Reconciliation .... Colossians 1:20
Anointing of the Sick .... James 5:14
(sacraments of healing)

This can be built individually or have two sets for team competition.

THE SEVEN UNITIES

Ephesians 4:4-6

One Church
One Spirit
One Hope
One Lord
One Faith
One Baptism
One God and Father of all

GOD LOVES YOU!!!!!!!
God wants you to know, love and serve Him
and be happy with Him in heaven!!!!!!!!

7

ENJOY HIS GOOD BOOK!
Will you walk with Jesus more closely
on our way to our heavenly home?